Chambers
card games for
gambling
great games for pleasure and profit

CHAMBERS
An imprint of Chambers Harrap Publishers Ltd
7 Hopetoun Crescent
Edinburgh
EH7 4AY

www.chambers.co.uk

First published by Chambers Harrap Publishers Ltd 2008

ISBN: 978 0550 10408 3

**Essex County
Council Libraries**

All gambling card games should be played responsibly. If you have any concerns,
the following organizations can be contacted for advice:

www.gamblersanonymous.org.uk and www.gambleaware.org.uk.

Designed by Chambers Harrap Publishers Ltd, Edinburgh
Typeset by Macmillan Publishing Solutions
Printed in Spain by Graphy Cems

Contributors

Author
Peter Arnold

Chambers Editor
Kate Sleight

Editorial Assistance
Alison Pickering

Prepress
Nico Echallier

Illustrations
Andrew Laycock
Macmillan Publishing Solutions

Publishing Manager
Hazel Norris

About the author

Peter Arnold is an author and editor, most of whose 50 or so books concern sports and games. He has written histories and encyclopedias of boxing, cricket, football and the Olympic Games, and wrote the official FIFA guide to the 1994 Football World Cup in the USA. He has also worked as editor and main contributor of part-works on boxing and football, and has ghost-written instruction books for a West Indian Test fast bowler and a Canadian world snooker champion.

Peter devised some of the mental games for the television series *The Crystal Maze*. Several of his books are on table games, including some on individual card games, and he has written three books on gambling, one of which was described by a New York author as 'the best history of gambling'. Many of his books have been published in the USA and in foreign-language editions.

Contents

Introduction..vii

Card Games

Ace-Deuce-Jack...3

All Fours...5

Baccarat...10

Bango..16

Banker...18

Blackjack..20

Blücher..26

Brag..28

Comet..34

Crazy Eights..37

Easy Go..39

Hoggenheimer..42

Lansquenet..45

Le Truc..48

Loo...51

Monte Bank...55

Napoleon..59

Newmarket..63

Ombre...66

Panguingue..71

Pinochle...75

Poker..81

Pontoon...99

Pope Joan..104

Preference..107

Racing...110

Red Dog...113

Schafkopf...116

Slippery Sam...120

Solo Whist..123

Spinado...128

Spoil Five...131

Stuss...135

Thirty-Five..137

Thirty-One..140

Trente et Quarante...142

More About Playing Cards

Card Games Basics..147

Card Games Glossary.......................................150

Customs, Practices and Etiquette.........................157

Card Sharp's Guide...159

Index

Games by Alternative Names...............................163

Games by Number of Players...............................164

Games by Type..166

Introduction by Peter Arnold

All games, not only card games, can be played for money merely by the players agreeing beforehand that the losers will pay the winners. So what defines a gambling game? A narrow definition would be a game decided by chance alone, with no element of skill. But that would be to exclude Poker, the most widely played of all games where money changes hands (indeed, it is a pointless game if not played for money). Poker is one of the most skilful of games, sometimes thought of more as money-management than a game of cards, so gambling games are not restricted to games of chance alone.

Looking up the word 'gamble' in the 2006 edition of *The Chambers Dictionary* would not encourage potential readers of this book; the entry reads as follows: '**Gamble** *vi* to play for money, especially for high stakes; to take a chance (with *on*); to engage in wild financial speculations; to take great risks for the sake of possible advantage * *vt* to squander or lose by staking * *n* a transaction depending on chance'. The expressions 'wild financial speculations', 'great risks' and 'squander or lose' have a whiff of disapproval about them, reminiscent of the 18th-century Puritans who called the pack of playing cards 'the devil's picture book' and banned it from their households.

This book takes a more relaxed view; the gambling games included here are a selection of those card games most suitable for betting, with stakes as high or low as the players may wish, with the emphasis on enjoyment rather than avarice, and certainly not on financial destruction or squandering. Some are simple games of pure chance and others demand various levels of skill or judgement.

The 36 games included cover a wide range. There are many ways of classifying them but three groups stand out, as follows:

Casino games The Baccarat family of games, with Blackjack and Trente et Quarante, are normally played in a casino, which provides the table and equipment necessary.

Banking games These are games where one of the players assumes the role of the banker, in effect taking over the role of the casino and playing against all the other players. In some of these games the banker has an advantage, ie would expect to show a profit over a long run. In these games it is necessary for fairness that each player should hold the bank as often as any other player. This is mentioned in the descriptions when applicable. Where there is no advantage to the banker, for example in games like Easy Go and Hoggenheimer, it should nevertheless be agreed that the bank should circulate. There are, however, players who do not wish to be banker, even when the game is biased in the banker's favour, and it is in order for a player to decline the bank. One game described, Slippery Sam, actually has a bias against the banker, and the bank is frequently lost. In this game all players must accept their turn as banker, and contribute to it an amount agreed in advance.

Pool games The most popular method of playing cards for money is by use of a pool. A pool, also known as a pot, or kitty, is a collection of stake money to which all players contribute, and which is shared out among the winners usually at the end of the game, although in some games the pool is taken from and added to while the game is in progress. There is a wide variety of pool games included in this book, such as the bingo-imitating Bango; the games of the Stops family, which includes Newmarket,

Pope Joan and Spinado; counting games such as Pontoon, Thirty-One and Thirty-Five and trick-taking games such as Loo, Preference and Spoil Five. Many of these are games in which skill plays a part.

In addition to games in the categories mentioned are a number which are not so easily classified. These include Brag and Poker, where players progressively bet on the value of their hands, Panguingue, a game of the Rummy family, Racing, which is based on horse-racing, Pinochle, a game of trick-taking and melding, and other trick-taking games, eg Napoleon and Solo Whist, where there is an auction.

All of the games included are, or have been, principally played for money. There are many other games in which players often have a financial interest, such as Bridge and Rummy, but these are usually played for their intrinsic merit alone and so are not included in this book. Reference may also be made to other games not featured, such as Bezique and Cinch, where the information is relevant or interesting; details of how to play these games can be found in *Chambers Card Games*.

Trick-taking There are ten games included in this book which involve trick-taking. In four of them the usual rules of trick-taking apply. These rules are set out in Card Games Basics on page 147. However, in six of the trick-taking games in this book (All Fours, Le Truc, Loo, Ombre, Pinochle and Spoil Five) there is a deviation from the normal rules. In each case the rules governing the trick-taking, and their exceptions from the norm, are carefully described. Where appropriate, example hands are included to make understanding easier.

Chips In a casino game, currency will not be used for betting. A player's money is converted into chips, which are tokens of plastic or a similar material, each representing a specific sum of money. These are used as stakes at the tables, and a player converts them back into currency when he stops playing. In the vast majority of private games, currency is used for betting. In rare cases where chips are used, particularly when different colours represent different amounts, players must be clear as to the value of each chip. In describing games it is easier and clearer to talk of stakes being of one, two, or five chips etc rather than pounds, euros or dollars.

It is always best when starting a session of gambling of any sort to decide on a limit you are prepared to lose, and to stop when that limit has been reached. It is the desperate attempt to regain losses which often leads to their acceleration and eventually to ultimate disaster, and it is this that led those Puritans to regard all gambling as sinful. Exercise discretion and enjoy the game.

Peter Arnold
London, March 2008

Card Games

Ace-Deuce-Jack

Ace-Deuce-Jack is a simple gambling game, requiring a banker. The game is so much in favour of the banker that it is usually encountered as a betting proposition suggested by a hustler, who proposes himself as the banker and enjoys a roughly ten per cent advantage over anybody he can persuade to bet with him.

Type	A simple gambling game of no skill played with a banker
Alternative names	None
Players	Two or more
Special requirements	Chips or cash for betting

Aim
To win money by betting that none of three cards turned up by cutting the pack is an Ace, 2 or Jack.

Cards
The standard pack of 52 cards is used, the cards ranking (for the purpose of deciding first banker) from Ace (high) to 2 (low).

Preparation
A minimum and maximum stake must be agreed beforehand.

Any player may pick up the cards and shuffle them. Another player cuts the cards, and deals a card to each. The player holding the highest card is the first banker. If there is a tie, a further card or cards are dealt to those tying until the tie is broken. Any player may then shuffle the cards, with the banker having the right to shuffle last. The cards are then cut by the player on the banker's right, and the cards returned to the banker.

Play
The banker removes three cards face down from the bottom of the pack and places them to one side. They take no part in the game. The banker places the remainder of the pack face down on the table, making sure that no player sees the denomination of the bottom card. The banker then makes two cuts placing the two piles cut from the pack alongside the remaining cards, so that the pack is divided into three piles in front of him. No player, including the banker, knows the denominations of the three cards at the bottom of the piles.

All players now place their bets by advancing towards the centre of the table a stake between the minimum and maximum allowed. They are betting that none of the three cards at the bottom of the piles is an Ace, 2 or Jack.

When all bets have been made, the banker turns face up the three piles to expose the cards previously at the bottom.

Settlement If none of the three cards exposed is an Ace, 2 or Jack, the players win and the banker pays each at even money, ie each player wins the amount of his stake. If one or more of the cards is an Ace, 2 or Jack, the banker wins and collects all the stakes.

The cards are then collected and passed to the player on the banker's left, who becomes the banker for the next deal. As the banker holds an advantage, the game should end only when all players have held the bank for an equal number of times.

The advantage to the bank can be calculated easily. From the players' point of view there are 12 losing cards – the Aces, 2s and Jacks. The remaining 40 cards are winning cards. The chance of the first exposed card *not* being an Ace, 2 or Jack is therefore 40 in 52 (the fact that three unknown cards have been cast aside does not affect the calculation). If it is not an Ace, 2 or Jack the chance of the second card not being an Ace, 2 or Jack is 39 in 51. The chance of the third card being a winning card is 38 in 50. The chance, therefore, of none of the cards being an Ace, 2 or Jack are those three chances multiplied together, which can be easily calculated to be 38 in 85. In other words, the banker will win 47 times to the players 38, or 55.3 per cent of all games, an advantage of just over ten per cent.

All Fours

All Fours is an ancient game from which others have been developed, such as California Jack, Cinch and Pitch. It is mentioned by Charles Cotton in *The Compleat Gamester*, published in 1674, as being popular in Kent and is referred to in *The Pickwick Papers* by Charles Dickens. It is a simple game which rewards careful play and is still popular as a recreational game played for amusement only. However in the USA in the 19th century, before the advent of Poker, it was a favourite medium of gambling, and it is for this reason that it is included in this book. The game described is played for points, with settlement coming at the end.

Type	A trick-taking game
Alternative names	High-Low-Jack, Old Sledge, Seven-Up
Players	Two; three or four for variants
Special requirements	Pen and paper for scoring, cash for betting

Aim
To win the game by scoring seven points; points are scored for capturing certain cards during tricks.

Cards
The standard pack of 52 cards is used, the cards ranking from Ace (high) to 2 (low).

Preparation
Players must agree the stakes, ie the amount per point the loser will pay for the difference in his score and the winner's score of seven.

Each player draws a card to determine the first dealer, the highest dealing. Thereafter each player deals in turn. The dealer shuffles the pack and the non-dealer cuts.

Each player is dealt six cards face down in two bundles of three, beginning with the non-dealer. The next card is turned up to indicate the trump suit. If it is a Jack, the dealer immediately scores one point.

Play
Begging When the deal has been made, the players look at their cards and the non-dealer has the option of either 'standing' or 'begging'. If he says 'I stand', the turn up is accepted as trumps and the trick-taking phase begins.

Alternatively, the trump card can be rejected, and the non-dealer instead says 'I beg'. This gives the dealer the option of accepting or rejecting the trump card. If the dealer accepts the trumps, he says 'Take one' and has to give the non-dealer one point for 'gift'. The trick-taking phase then begins.

However, if the dealer also does not like the trump card, he says 'I refuse the gift' or 'I run the cards', which mean the same. Remember that if the non-dealer has six points, needing one to win the game, the dealer must always refuse the gift; otherwise he would lose immediately.

Running the cards When the dealer runs the cards, the rejected turn up is discarded face down and each player is dealt another bundle of three cards face down, turning up the next card. If it is different from the rejected trump card, it becomes trumps. If, however, it is the same suit as the rejected trump suit, it too is discarded face down as are the two bundles of three cards, without the players looking at them. A further three cards are dealt to each hand and a third face-up card is dealt to indicate trumps. If necessary, this exercise is repeated until a new trump suit is established (in the unlikely event of the pack being exhausted without the trump suit being established, the deal is abandoned). If the card establishing the new trump suit is a Jack, the dealer scores one point. (The dealer does not score a point if in running the cards the Jack of the rejected trump suit is turned up.)

The new trump suit cannot be rejected, and once it is established the players pick up the three new cards they have been dealt and add them to their hands. They now each hold nine cards and have to reduce their hands to six by discarding three face down.

Trick-taking The trick-taking phase now begins, with the non-dealer leading to the first of the six tricks; see p148 for an explanation of tricks and trick-taking. A trick is won, as usual, by the higher trump it contains or the higher card of the suit led. In a departure from most trick-taking games, the second player is allowed to trump even if able to follow suit. The player cannot discard, however, if a card of the suit led is held – the player must either follow suit or trump. If unable to follow suit, the player can trump or discard as desired. If trumps are led, the second player must follow suit, if able to. The winner of a trick leads to the next.

When all six tricks have been played the scores are calculated in the order below.

Scoring Four main points are at stake in each deal, hence the name All Fours. The four points are scored as follows:

High　for winning the highest trump in play;

Low　for winning the lowest trump in play;

Jack　for winning the Jack of trumps, if in play;

Game　for winning the highest value of scoring cards in tricks, the scoring scale being

Ace	4
King	3
Queen	2
Jack	1
10	10

If the players have an equal count the non-dealer scores the point.

Of course the player dealt the highest trump in play must win the point for High, since he must win a trick with it. If there is only one trump in play it wins the point for both High and Low. Similarly, if the Jack of trumps is highest or lowest trump, it wins the point for High or Low as well as for Jack, and could in fact win all three points. If the Jack is not in play, the point for Jack is not scored, meaning that only three main points are scored in that deal.

The winner is the first to seven points, the main points after each deal being taken in the order High, Low, Jack, Game, except when Jack is turned up as the trump indicator, in which case the dealer scores for it immediately. Another point can be scored immediately during the deal for gift, as explained above.

It sometimes happens that a player will 'count out' during a deal (for example, if a player on six points holds the Ace of trumps, he must win the point for High, which is counted first, and therefore must win). In that case, the deal is not played out.

Settlement Once a player has reached seven points, no further points are taken, eg if a player reaches seven points with a point for Low, the points for Jack and Game are not taken, irrespective of which player captured the Jack, or has accumulated the necessary points for Game. The final score is always therefore seven points for the winner and a smaller number for the loser. The loser pays the winner according to the difference in the scores, at the agreed sum per point.

Example hand
The cards are dealt as shown in the illustration, with ♣4 turned up to indicate the trump suit.

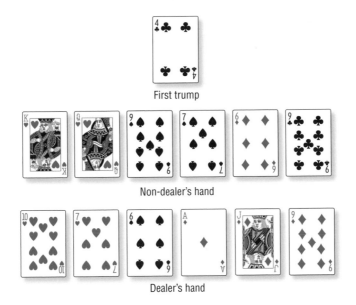

First trump

Non-dealer's hand

Dealer's hand

After the deal the non-dealer begs, as he holds only one middling club. The dealer, who holds no trumps, refuses the gift and runs the cards as illustrated overleaf.

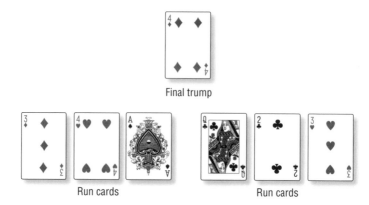

Final trump

Run cards   Run cards

Diamonds is the new trump suit, and the players pick up their extra three cards. Diamonds is excellent for the dealer, as he already holds ♦A, J, 9. With these he keeps ♥10, 7, 3. His policy is to lead hearts and hope to make at least ♦A, J and ♥10, which should ensure he gains at least three, and probably four, points. The non-dealer keeps ♦6, 3, ♠A, 9, ♥K, Q. The final hand of each player is shown below.

Non-dealer's final hand

Dealer's final hand

The non-dealer leads to the first trick and play proceeds as follows:

	Non-dealer	Dealer
1	♠9	♦J
2	♦3	♥3
3	♠A	♦9
4	♥K	♥7
5	♥Q	♦A
6	♦6	♥10

On the first lead, the dealer made sure of a point by playing the Jack of trumps, and followed his policy by leading ♥3. The non-dealer, instead of winning the trick with his ♥K, decided to trump with ♦3, which would be likely to gain him a point for Low. He then led ♠A, which the dealer took with ♦9, leading another heart, which this time drew ♥K. Now the non-dealer led his last heart, which the dealer trumped with Ace, and then led his ♥10, expecting it to win. Unfortunately, the non-dealer had a trump left and won the last trick.

So the deal ended at two points each, with the dealer scoring for High and Jack, and the non-dealer for Low and Game, his count for the game being 13 to 11.

Where the dealer, who had much the better hand, went wrong, was not so much in his play of the cards but in the choice of his hand. He would have done better to have discarded the ♥10, because no matter what other cards he held with his three trumps, he would have won the point for Game.

Variants

In the original game of All Fours, the point for Low was awarded to the player who held the lowest trump in the deal, rather than to the player who won it in the trick-taking phase, and in many books this is still how the game is described. However, the game is obviously better if the point is awarded to the player winning the card, rather than to the one fortuitously dealt it, and that is how modern players play it, and how the game is described above; some books might describe the above game as a descendant of the original game.

Settlement variation Rather than play the game to seven points, scoring with pencil and paper can be dispensed with altogether by treating each deal as a separate entity, with each time a point is won, the loser paying the winner the agreed stake immediately. This means that all deals are played to a finish, and the convention of not completing a deal when one player reaches seven does not apply. This is the method of settlement preferred by gamblers.

Three-handed All Fours In this variation there are three players, who play as individuals. Only the dealer and the eldest hand (the player on the dealer's left) look at their cards after the deal. The eldest hand has the option of standing or begging, as described, and the dealer of playing with the original trump or running the cards. Only when the trump is established does the third player pick up his cards. If the cards have been run, all players reduce their hands to six cards and play proceeds as above.

When there is a tie in the count for Game, if it is between the dealer and a non-dealer, the non-dealer gets the point; if between the two non-dealers the point for game is not scored.

Settlement is continuous. Every time a player scores a point the other two pay him the agreed stake. The game should not end until each player has been dealer the same number of times.

Four-handed All Fours This variation for four players is played in two partnerships, partners sitting opposite each other. The dealer and the eldest hand only take part in the determination of the trump suit. The other players do not pick up their hands until the trick-taking phase begins when all players, if necessary, reduce their hands to six cards. The partners' tricks are combined for scoring purposes, so scoring is the same as in the two-handed game.

Settlement is continuous. Each time a team wins a point, each member of the team receives the agreed stake, one from one member of the losing team and the other from the other loser.

Baccarat

Baccarat is the ultimate gambling game, at which in the golden days of the casinos at Deauville and Monte Carlo in the 1920s fortunes were literally made and lost on the turn of a single card. It is a very simple game, of practically no skill, designed to redistribute vast sums of wealth quickly in casinos. Invented in France in the 19th century, it became popular in casinos and was played by the rich and aristocratic, thus gaining a glamorous image.

Baccarat is basically a two-handed game, between the banker (also the dealer) and the non-dealer. In the basic game described, the casino provides the bank and the banker. The players, who bet against the bank, do not take an active part in the game, except for one who acts for them as a whole, usually the player who has made the biggest bet. The game is often called Baccarat-banque, because the casino is the bank and provides the dealer, or Baccarat à deux tableaux, because the dealer plays against two other hands simultaneously, represented by tableau one and tableau two.

Type	Game of chance played in casinos
Alternative names	Baccara, Chemin de Fer, Punto Banco
Players	Up to twelve
Special requirements	Played in a casino, which provides the venue, table, cards, chips and the croupier

Aim
To hold a hand of a higher point value than that of the banker.

Cards
Six standard packs of 52 cards are normally used.

Preparation
The players seat themselves around the table in the twelve numbered places. If more wish to play they stand behind those seated. The banker and a croupier (who deals with the disposal of stakes and cards) sit or stand as shown opposite.

After shuffling, the cards are placed in a *sabot*, or dealing shoe, with a marker placed before the tenth card from the back, these last cards not being used.

Players may bet that tableau 1, tableau 2 or both will beat the banker. Stakes are placed in the spaces marked 1 or 2 on the table respectively. The croupier will place stakes for players who cannot reach the appropriate space. A player may bet that both tableaux will beat the banker, and the stake for this is placed on the line between 1 and 2; the player wins if both tableaux beat the banker, loses if both lose and retains his stake if one wins and the other loses. This bet is called à *cheval*.

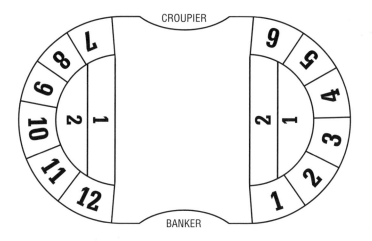

Play

When all bets are placed, the dealer deals one card at a time face down from the sabot, beginning with tableau 1 (to his right) then tableau 2 (to his left) and then to himself, until all three hands consist of two cards.

All cards count their pip value, with Ace counting one and court cards ten. The values of the two cards are added together to obtain a 'point', but if the value exceeds ten, the second digit only of the sum counts as the point. Thus a 7 and 6, which equal 13, count as a point of 3. A King and a 5 give a point of 5 (10+5 = 15), a 6 and a 4 a point of zero. The highest point possible is therefore 9.

A two-card hand with a point of 9 is known in French as *le grand*, and is the best hand possible. A two-card hand with a point of 8 is *le petit*, which beats everything except *le grand*. British and US players call these hands 'naturals' – natural 9 and natural 8.

In certain circumstances, described below, a player or banker will draw a third card, his point being calculated in the same way, by adding the values of the three cards and taking the second digit, if necessary.

Once the initial cards have been dealt, the players representing each tableau and the banker then look at their cards, and if any holds a natural 9 or 8 the hand is exposed, since these cannot be beaten, and wins immediately (except that, of course, a natural 8 loses to a natural 9). Otherwise the hands are replaced face down.

If the banker does not have a natural, he must deal in turn with the two hands against him, beginning with tableau 1. The player representing tableau 1 must state whether he wishes to stand with the point he has, or draw a third card. With all points except 5 he has no choice (he is, of course, only representative of all the players who have bet on tableau 1). He must choose to stand with a point of 6 or 7 and draw with a point of 0, 1, 2, 3 or 4. This has been worked out as the best strategy, anyway, and is called the Table of Play. Only with a point of 5 has he a choice; it has been estimated that it is slightly better in this situation to stand than to draw.

A player who draws a third card has this dealt face up, but leaves the two cards previously dealt to him face down on the table, so only he knows his final point.

Having dealt with tableau 1, the banker repeats the process with tableau 2, and then must consider his own hand. The banker also has a Table of Play which, like that for the player, sets out the optimum play, but in his case it can only be advisory, since the banker is playing against two opponents at once, and the Table of Play might indicate drawing against one and standing against the other. In practice, of course, the banker will estimate which tableau is carrying the higher stake, and follow the Table of Play as if playing against that hand only. The banker's Table of Play is set out here, and applies also to the Chemin de Fer variant which follows.

Banker's Table of Play for Baccarat and Chemin de Fer

Banker's point	Banker draws if player draws	Banker stands if player draws	Banker has option if player draws
3	0, 1, 2, 3, 4, 5, 6, 7	8	9
4	2, 3, 4, 5, 6, 7	0, 1, 8, 9	–
5	5, 6, 7	0, 1, 2, 3, 8, 9	4
6	6, 7	0, 1, 2, 3, 4, 5, 8, 9	–

Note: The banker always draws on 0, 1 and 2, stands on 7 and exposes a natural on 8 or 9. If the player does not draw, the banker is advised to stand on 6 and draw on 3, 4 and 5.

When all hands are complete, with either two or three cards, they are exposed, and the players win or lose according to whether their point is higher or lower than the banker's. The side, banker or player, with the higher point is the winner, with the proviso that a natural 9 or 8 beats any three-card point. If they win, they win the amount of their stake, and if they lose, they lose their stake. Where the banker's and player's hands are equal, the player retains his stake.

Variants

Chemin de Fer Chemin de Fer is played in casinos on a table with a different layout. The main difference from the parent game is that the players themselves hold the bank in turn, with the casino charging a commission. This is the version of the game most suitable for play at home, as it can be managed without the refinements of the casino table and the croupier to manage the settlement of the bets. In a casino the sabot is passed round the table, stopping at each player as a train might at each station, hence the name Chemin de Fer, the French for 'railway'. The sabot will usually contain at least six packs with a marker placed towards the back so that not all are used. For games among friends at home, of course, a single pack shuffled after each deal might be regarded as acceptable.

The first banker can be chosen in two ways. Either the player willing to put up the biggest bank becomes the banker, or the banker can be chosen by lot, whichever the players prefer. The banker places the amount of the bank before him.

The game is a straight two-handed contest between banker and players. The players place their stakes in front of them, beginning with the player to the banker's right. That player may bet any amount, up to the amount of the bank. The next player

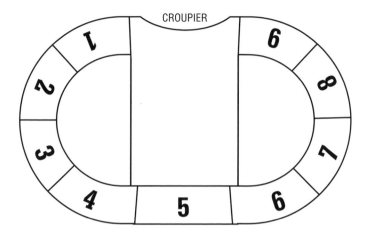

does likewise and so on until the total of the players' stakes is equal to the bank. It follows that some players may not get the chance to bet on every hand. If when all players have made their bets the amount in the bank is not covered, the surplus is removed by the banker.

There are, however, three 'preferential' bets allowed. Before the deal any player may call '*banco*', which allows that player to bet the whole of the amount in the bank himself. If two or more players wish to call banco, the precedence goes to the player nearest to the banker's right. The second preferential call, which has precedence over all others, operates only after a call of banco. If the caller loses his bet and the banker collects the stake, which thereby doubles the size of the bank, the loser is entitled to call '*banco suivi*', which allows him to bet the whole amount of the bank again. After this he may call banco again, but his status is only that of the other players.

The third preferential call, and the third in rank, is '*avec la table*'. This allows the caller to bet half the value of the bank, the other players being at liberty to bet the remainder as normal.

When all bets are made the banker deals the two hands face down, one card at a time, to players and himself alternately, so that both hands are of two cards. The player placing the highest stake holds the cards for players.

As described in Baccarat, above, the aim is to have the highest point, ie that closest to 9. Banker and player look at their hands and expose them if a natural 8 or 9 is held, which settles bets immediately. Otherwise, the rules for standing or drawing apply as for Baccarat, ie the player drawing with 0, 1, 2, 3 or 4, standing with 6 or 7 and having the option with 5, while the banker must then stand or draw according to the Table of Play set out above. However, there is one exception, which occurs when 'banco' or 'banco suivi' has been called. It arises from the fact that the player in these cases is playing only for himself and not for all the players as a group. In this case, some casinos allow both player and banker to ignore the rules and draw or stand at their discretion, a practice known as '*faux tirages*', or 'false draws'. Players in private games must decide in advance whether to allow them.

As in Baccarat, when the hands are complete they are compared, and if the players win they are paid from the bank, which eliminates it, or they pay the bank, which doubles it. When the bank is eliminated the player to the right of the banker becomes the new banker, if he wishes, and places an amount on the table to form the bank. If that player declines to be the banker, the bank passes to the player to the right and so on.

A banker who wins can either withdraw the bank with his winnings and pass the opportunity to be banker to the right, or retain the bank, in which case the whole of it remains for the next deal. The player is not allowed to withdraw part of it and carry on with the rest, unless in a casino and the bank exceeds the casino's limit.

Punto Banco Punto Banco is a simplified version of Chemin de Fer that is popular in casinos. It is an automatic game of chance with no options at all. Up to twelve players sit at spaces marked, and there are two spaces for croupiers. One croupier deals and the other plays the players' hand. Each player in turn is given the opportunity to play the banker's hand. Thus the names 'players' and 'bank' have no significance other than to give a name to the two hands. Nobody is required to put up a bank and players make the simple choice of which side will win; they will either lose their stake to the casino or be paid out by the casino accordingly.

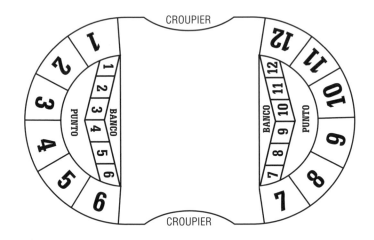

A player makes bets by placing a stake of any amount between the casino's limits in the spaces provided. A bet on *punto*, or players (in some casinos the table is marked 'players' instead of 'punto'), is placed in the big numbered box before him, while a bet on banco, or bank, is placed in the smaller box corresponding to his number.

A croupier deals from a sabot the two hands of two cards, one at a time. The players' hand is dealt to the croupier opposite and the bank's hand to the player whose turn it is to play it. As in the two versions described above, the aim is to obtain the closest point value to 9. However, neither side has any options, and both must obey the Table of Play:

Player's Table of Play for Punto Banco

Point

0, 1, 2, 3, 4, 5	Draws
6, 7	Stands
8, 9	Exposes cards

Banker's Table of Play for Punto Banco

Point	Draws if player draws	Stands if player draws
0, 1, 2	0, 1, 2, 3, 4, 5, 6, 7, 8, 9	
3	0, 1, 2, 3, 4, 5, 6, 7, 9	8
4	2, 3, 4, 5, 6, 7	0, 1, 8, 9
5	4, 5, 6, 7	0, 1, 2, 3, 8, 9
6	6, 7	0, 1, 2, 3, 4, 5, 8, 9
7	Stands	
8, 9	Exposes cards	

Note: If the player does not draw, banker draws on 0, 1, 2, 3, 4 and 5, stands on 6 and 7, and exposes his cards on 8 and 9.

Bets are settled when both hands are completed. Bets on punto, or players, are settled at a straightforward even money, or 1–1, but on banco, or bank, at odds of 19–20 ie at 5% less than 1–1. It has been estimated that the bank hand has a 1.34% advantage over the players' hand when the likelihood of it winning is calculated, which means that players betting on the players' hand are conceding the casino a 1.34% edge, while those betting on the bank hand are conceding 1.20%. The bank hand is therefore the slightly better bet.

Bango

Bango was invented when the game of bingo became a craze in Great Britain in the 1960s, and is an attempt to use playing cards to bring some of the atmosphere of the bingo hall to the home. It is necessarily played for smaller stakes but is a fair game of pure luck with equal chances of winning or losing over a long period. Children could play this game.

Type	A playing card version of bingo, with no skill involved
Alternative names	None
Players	Three to ten, the more the better; for more than ten, see variant
Special requirements	Money or chips for betting; a bowl or saucer to hold the pool of stakes

Aim
Each player aims to win by being the first to turn all his face-up cards face down.

Cards
Two standard packs of 52 cards are required for up to ten players. It is convenient if the packs have different backs, as they should not be mixed.

Preparation
Any player may pick up one pack of cards and shuffle. Another cuts and deals one card face up to each player to decide the first dealer – the player who receives the first Jack is the first dealer. There is no advantage or disadvantage to being the dealer.

Each player puts an agreed amount into the bowl to form a pool. The dealer and the player to his left each shuffle a pack of cards, and the player to the dealer's right cuts each pack.

Play
The dealer takes one pack and deals the cards singly to each player, including himself, until each has five cards. The players arrange their cards face up in a row before them. The dealer then puts the first pack aside.

The dealer then takes the second pack of cards and deals the top card face up to the table, announcing its rank and suit. If any player, including the dealer, has among the cards in front of him the card from the first pack which matches the dealt card in both rank and suit he turns his card face down.

The dealer then deals the second card face up to the table, announcing it in the same manner, and a player whose cards include the identical card from the first pack turns it face down, and so on.

As soon as a player has turned over all five of his cards, he calls 'Bango'. The dealer then checks that all the turned-over cards have their match among the cards he dealt. The first player to turn over all five of his cards takes the pool.

Variants

If there are more than ten players, then a third pack must be employed. Two packs with identical backs are required to deal out the players' hands, while the third pack, with a different back, is used for the dealer to indicate the winning cards.

It may be that a player's hand, when two packs are used to provide it, may include two identical cards, but this does not matter. If the matching card is turned up by the dealer, the player turns face down both of his identical cards.

It could happen, but rarely, that two players could call 'Bango' at the same time. In this case they share the pool.

Banker

Banker is the simplest of all gambling games, with the outcome depending solely on whether the player's card is of a higher or lower rank than that of the banker. There are slight variations of procedure.

Type	A simple gambling game where chance rules
Alternative names	Blind Hookey, Dutch Bank
Players	Two or more
Special requirements	Chips or cash for betting

Aim
To hold a card of higher denomination than that held by the banker.

Cards
The standard pack of 52 cards is used, the cards ranking from Ace (high) to 2 (low).

Preparation
A minimum and maximum stake must be agreed beforehand.

Players cut the deck, with the player cutting the highest card (Ace high) being the first banker. If there is a tie, the tied players cut again to decide precedence. Any player may then shuffle the cards, but the banker has the option to shuffle last. The player to the banker's right cuts the cards.

Play
The banker places the pack face down in front of him and cuts a number of piles from the deck, one for each player and the last for himself. The remainder of the pack is placed to one side and does not come into play.

The players place their bets beside their piles.

Settlement The banker turns over his pile to reveal face up the card previously at the bottom. He then turns over the pile of each player in turn. If the player's face-up card is of a higher rank than that of the banker, the banker pays the player the amount of his stake. If the player's card is lower, the banker collects the stake. If the cards are of equal rank, the player retains his stake.

When all bets are settled, the cards are collected up and the player to the banker's left becomes banker for the next deal.

Variants
Instead of cutting a pile for each player, the banker may cut only three piles in total: two for the players, however many there might be, and one for himself. The players may bet on whichever players' pile they choose. Or the banker may deal any

number of players' piles. The players may bet on whichever pile they wish – some piles may be left without being bet upon (these are not turned face up during the settlement).

Some players prefer that when the player's and banker's cards are equal, the banker wins the stake, rather than the player retaining it. As this gives the banker an advantage, it is essential that all players hold the bank an equal number of times.

Instead of leaving part of the pack unused, the banker may instead remove just the bottom card from the pack and place it to one side. The object in both cases is to ensure that no player knows the value of the bottom card of the banker's pile.

Instead of the bank passing on each hand, each banker holds the bank an agreed number of times. The bank may not pass on rotation, but be cut for on each change. Or the bank may pass only to a player who wins a bet with an Ace (if two or more players win with an Ace on the same deal, they cut for it).

Needless to say, if any of these variants are to be employed, all players must agree to them before play begins.

Blackjack

Blackjack got its name when a US casino, in order to advertise the game known as Twenty-One, offered a bonus to any player holding a winning hand consisting of an Ace of spades with either of the black Jacks. This hand became known as a 'blackjack', which quickly became the name for the game itself. It is the streamlined version of the game known originally (and in France, still) as Vingt-et-Un and in the UK as Pontoon. Pontoon is better for private play, the casino version being much more mechanical.

Type	Game requiring judgement, played in casinos
Alternative names	None; Vingt-et-Un, Pontoon and Twenty-One are alternative names of the domestic games of which Blackjack is a version
Players	Any number against the bank; a casino table often has space for seven players
Special requirements	Played in a casino, which provides the venue, table, cards, chips and the croupier (banker)

Aim
To hold a hand of higher point value than that of the banker.

Cards
Four standard packs of 52 cards are used. Plain cards have their pip value, and court cards each count as ten. Aces, when held by a player, have a value of one or eleven, according to the player's discretion. An Ace has the same dual value when held by the banker, but with limits, as described below.

Preparation
Players sit round the roughly semi-circular table as illustrated, facing the banker. If space is available at the tables a player may occupy two adjacent spaces and

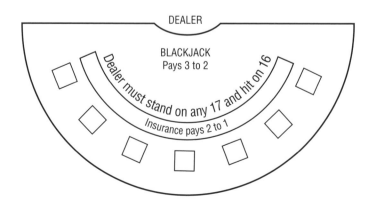

operate two hands against the banker. The two hands are entirely separate, and a player plays out one before he plays out the other.

The cards are shuffled together by the banker. Any player may cut by inserting an indicator card into the face-down pack. The cut is completed by the banker who reverses the positions of the cards below and above the indicator, removing the indicator card. The pack is placed face down in a *sabot*, or dealing shoe, and the indicator card is inserted some 50 cards from the end of the pack. When this is reached during play, the deal in which it occurs will be completed, but no further deals will be made with this pack, the cards remaining in the sabot not being used.

Players first of all place a stake, which can be of any amount within the minimum and maximum limits of the casino (or, indeed, the table, since casinos may have tables with differing limits). The stake is placed in the rectangle marked on the table in front of each player.

Play

The banker deals and 'burns' the first card dealt from the sabot, ie discards it without its value being shown.

Then, beginning with the player sitting to his extreme left, the banker deals a card in turn face up to all players, including himself. He then deals a second card to each, face up in the players' cases, and face down in his.

The player's object is to obtain a hand, with two or more cards, with a point count higher than that of the banker, without exceeding a maximum of 21. Should his count exceed 21 he has 'busted', and loses his stake.

A count of 21 with two cards, ie an Ace and a ten-point card, is known as a 'blackjack' or 'natural', and beats all other hands. (Note that a blackjack is now any two-card count of 21, and a Jack, either black or red, is not an essential part of it.) When a player wins with a blackjack, the bank pays him at odds of 3–2, which is usually stated on the table layout. Otherwise, bets are settled at odds of 1–1. If the player's and banker's hands are tied, neither wins, and the player retains his stake.

If the banker has a blackjack, he wins all the stakes immediately, except those from a player who also has a blackjack, in which case there is a tie. If the banker's face-up card is an Ace or a ten-count card, he looks at his face-down card and, if it gives him a blackjack, he reveals it and collects the players' stakes without further ado. If not, he replaces the card face-down and play continues. If the banker's face-up card is an Ace, however, he offers the players the opportunity to insure against his holding a blackjack. A player who wishes to insure places a premium of half his stake in the betting space before him. The banker then looks at his face-down card, and if it gives him a blackjack he declares it. Players who insured are paid at odds of 2–1 (this will be stated on the blackjack table itself) on their premium, so receive on the insurance the stake they lost on the play. In practice, they retain their stake and their premium and neither lose nor win on the deal. Players who did not insure, of course, lose their stakes. Should the banker not have a blackjack, he returns his card face-down to his hand, and play proceeds as usual, with players who insured losing their premium but remaining in the game. The banker now deals with all the players in turn, beginning with the player on his extreme left.

Each player has three options (plus a fourth should his two cards be of equal rank). They are to:

Stand   This means that he is satisfied with his hand as it is, and does not wish to try to improve it. He will usually be satisfied with a total of 19, 20 or 21.

Draw   A player not happy with his count may ask the banker to deal him additional cards until he is. This is often done by tapping his cards and saying 'Hit me'. Thus 'to hit' has become a term meaning to draw a card. Should the player receive a card when drawing which takes his count over 21, he busts and loses his stake. The banker will collect his stake immediately and dispose of his cards.

Split   A player dealt two cards of the same rank (in this respect all cards which count ten are regarded as being of the same rank) may split them. He separates the two cards, which become the first cards of two separate hands. The player puts a second stake, equal to his original stake, on the second hand. The banker then deals him a second card to each hand, and each hand is then dealt with in turn, beginning with the one to the player's right. The player has the same choices with split hands as with any other hand (including the opportunity to split either hand further, should the second card dealt to it be of the same rank as the first) with one exception. Should he split a pair of Aces, the second card dealt to each hand completes it (unless it is another Ace, when he may split again). If splitting Aces, he cannot draw a third card to the hand. This means, in practice, that Aces in split hands count as eleven and not one. The count of a hand which does not contain an Ace, or which counts an Ace as one, is known as a 'hard' count, whereas a count in which an Ace is counted as eleven is a 'soft' count. A blackjack occurring in a split hand wins, of course, but is paid at the usual odds of 1–1 instead of the special blackjack odds of 3–2.

Double down A player may double his stake and receive a third card face down. This completes the hand, and the card remains face down until the banker faces it when settling.

The optimum strategies for players are detailed in the table opposite.

When the banker has dealt with each player and, in the case of those who busted, collected their stakes and disposed of their cards, he exposes his face-down card. He has no options in playing his hand. If his total count is 17, 18, 19 or 20 he must stand, if it is 16 or fewer he must draw and continue to draw until it reaches 17 to 21, when he must stand. If while drawing his count exceeds 21, he busts and pays out to all players still in the game.

An Ace can still count as one or eleven for the banker but he has no control over it. For example, if his hand is A, 4 and if his third card is a 9, he then has a hard 14, counting Ace as one, and must draw again. On the other hand, if his third card was a 2, he would have a soft 17 and he must therefore stand on 17. He cannot regard his hand as a hard 7 and draw again, as he would do if he had the choice and all the players had counts of 18 or more.

When the banker stands, he pays all players with a higher count than him and collects the stakes of those with a lower count. Players who tie retain their stakes and neither win nor lose.

Strategy This book is not meant for professional gamblers who might spend their lives trying to beat the casino at Blackjack by sophisticated methods of card counting – logging the ranks of the cards played to assess which remain and betting accordingly – but as mathematicians have worked out the optimum play for all situations, it would be useful to include the methods here.

With best play, the casino edge (the percentage of the stakes it would expect to win over the long run) is low – less than 1%. The casino has the advantage, despite the player having all the options in the game, and a tie being a stand-off, with neither side winning. The casino's advantage cancels out all others: the banker plays second. When a player busts, he loses. When the banker busts, he loses only to those players who haven't already bust. In this respect a tie isn't a stand-off – if player and banker both bust, banker wins.

A player's main choice is whether to stand, be hit or double down. The accompanying table sets out what most accept as the best options.

Player's optimum play at Blackjack

Player holds	Dealer's face-up card									
	2	3	4	5	6	7	8	9	10	A
Hard 17	S	S	S	S	S	S	S	S	S	S
2-card 16	S	S	S	S	S	H	H	H	S	S
Total 15	S	S	S	S	S	H	H	H	H	H
14	S	S	S	S	S	H	H	H	H	H
13	S	S	S	S	S	H	H	H	H	H
12	H	H	S	S	S	H	H	H	H	H
11	D	D	D	D	D	D	D	D	D	D
10	D	D	D	D	D	D	D	D	H	H
9	D	D	D	D	D	H	H	H	H	H
Soft 19	S	S	S	S	S	S	S	S	S	S
2-card 18	S	S	S	S	S	S	H	H	H	H
total 17	D	D	D	D	D	H	H	H	H	H
16	H	H	H	H	D	H	H	H	H	H
15	H	H	H	H	D	H	H	H	H	H
14	H	H	H	H	D	H	H	H	H	H
13	H	H	H	H	D	H	H	H	H	H

S = stand, H = hit, D = double down.

Note: always stand on hard hands of 17 or more and soft hands of 19 and 20.

A further choice confronts a player who holds a pair of cards of equal rank. The accompanying table is a consensus of expert opinion on whether he should split his pair:

Advisability of splitting pairs

Player's pair	Dealer's face-up card									
	2	3	4	5	6	7	8	9	10	A
A	S	S	S	S	S	S	S	S	S	S
10	X	X	X	X	X	X	X	X	X	X
9	S	S	S	S	S	X	X	X	X	X
8	S	S	S	S	S	S	S	X	X	S
7	S	S	S	S	S	S	X	X	X	X
6	S	S	S	S	S	X	X	X	X	X
5	X	X	X	X	X	X	X	X	X	X
4	X	X	X	X	X	X	X	X	X	X
3	S	S	S	S	S	S	X	X	X	X
2	S	S	S	S	S	S	X	X	X	X

S = split, X = do not split.

When it comes to the choice of whether or not to take insurance, the advice is incontestably 'no'. Insurance is really a bet. It is a bet that when the banker's face-up card is an Ace, his face-down card will be of a ten-count. Card-counting aside, the proportion of ten-counts in the pack is 16 to 36. The actual odds against a blackjack, therefore, are 9–4, while the odds offered by the casino are 2–1, a casino edge of over 7%. To be fair to casinos, however, the edge is possibly modest compared to that of real insurance companies charging premiums on policies for more everyday risks.

Variants

Casinos around the world might not operate the game exactly as described above. Variants which might be encountered include:

i) Bankers will draw on soft 17. This will be a rule, and will be stated. Bankers should never have options, since they are playing against several players, and what might favour them against one player might disfavour them against another.

ii) Players' initial cards will be dealt face down. This does not affect the game.

iii) Doubling down might be restricted, say, to hands of a count of eleven only, or to ten and eleven, or nine, ten and eleven.

iv) Insurance will not be offered, or will be offered only to a player holding blackjack.

v) Splitting pairs of 4, 5, or 10 will be barred.

vi) The banker will not deal a second card to himself until he has dealt with all the other hands and betting is completed.

All these variants except the last are harmless and tend to follow the optimum play for players. The last, like some of the others, was introduced by the Gaming Board of Great Britain to prevent collusion between the banker and a player or players. It means that players might double down when the banker's hand turns out to be a blackjack, and thereby lose stakes which otherwise would be saved. It gives the banker an extra advantage, and it also skews the tables of optimum play, making it inadvisable when the banker's first card is an Ace or ten-count to double down at all, or to split any pairs but Aces.

Blücher

As well as being a bid in the game of Napoleon, Blücher is also the name of a rather sedate gambling game. In both cases the name comes from the Prussian general who helped Wellington beat Napoleon at Waterloo.

Type	An unusual gambling game with a banker
Alternative names	None
Players	Three or more, the more the better
Special requirements	Thirteen cards, one of each rank, from another pack, or a drawn layout representing cards; chips or cash for betting

Aim
To bet on a rank of card that is not matched by the dealer during play.

Cards
The standard pack of 52 cards is used, the cards ranking (for the purpose of deciding the first banker) from Ace (high) to 2 (low). However, one card of each rank from a separate pack can be used as a betting layout – otherwise a layout showing each of the 13 ranks must be made to enable players to bet. Bets are made on any of the ranks of cards.

Preparation
A betting layout is made ideally by laying out in a row in the centre of the table one card of each rank from a spare pack of cards. Otherwise the ranks must be drawn on a layout.

All players draw a card from a spread pack, the highest card drawn (Ace high) determines the first banker. If there is a tie, those who tie draw again. The banker holds the bank for one deal, which subsequently passes to the left. Play should continue until each player has held the bank an equal number of times.

A minimum and maximum betting stake must be agreed beforehand. All players apart from the banker may place bets on any rank of card. Bets are governed by the agreed limits, but players may bet on as many ranks of card as they wish, and more than one player may bet on the same card. Each single bet is on one rank of card only, ie players cannot bet on a pair of cards or any other combination of cards. Bets cannot be changed, added to or removed when play has begun.

Once the bets have been made, any player may shuffle the cards, but the banker has the option of shuffling last. The player to the banker's right then cuts the cards.

Play
The banker takes the pack face down in his hand and deals the cards one at a time face up to the table. As he deals the first he calls 'Ace', the second he calls '2', the

third '3' and so on. For the eleventh he calls 'Jack', for the twelfth 'Queen' and for the thirteenth 'King'. If the card he turns over matches the rank that he calls out, then the banker wins the stakes on that card, plus an additional equal amount added to them by the player or players who bet on the card.

When the banker reaches 'King', he repeats the sequence again, calling 'Ace' for the fourteenth card, and so on. When the pack is exhausted, he will have run through the Ace to King sequence four times, collecting the stakes on the relevant cards, plus the additional amount, each time his call matches the turn-up.

However, the banker's job is not only to collect when he wins. If, during the course of turning cards over from the pack, one of his Ace to King sequences does not produce a match, he must double all the stakes remaining on the layout. He has to do this only once during a deal. If by chance he should suffer a second or third sequence of Ace to King without a match, he does not have to redouble the stakes. A match is always valid, ie it is a match even if there are no stakes on the rank matched, or if it is the second, third or fourth time the same rank has been matched.

When the stakes are doubled, the procedure remains the same. Each time the banker's call matches the rank of the card he turns over, he collects the doubled stakes on that card, plus an equal amount from the player or players who placed the stakes there.

Settlement When the banker has dealt all the cards to the table, and has collected on the way all the losing stakes from the layout, the players take back any of their stakes that remain on the layout. If the banker has not suffered an Ace to King sequence without a match, then of course the players merely get back their stakes without profit, but if the banker has had to double the stakes then they each show a profit equal to their stake.

Brag

Brag is one of the oldest card games, although the way it is played has changed radically over the centuries. Games of cards on which players bet on the value of the hands they hold have been played everywhere in the world, with the 16th-century Italian game of Primiera often cited as the root from which grew both Brag and Poker. Primero, as it was known in England, is mentioned by Shakespeare as having been played by Henry VIII, and was a favourite of Elizabeth I. It is related to Poker, which in the past few years has overtaken it completely.

The game described, known as Modern Brag, is a version that is played popularly today. The classical game, now practically extinct, is described here as a variant.

Type	Game where judgement can be exercised in betting
Alternative names	None
Players	Any reasonable number; four to eight is best
Special requirements	Chips or cash for staking

Aim
To hold a better hand than that of the other players.

Cards
The standard pack of 52 cards is used, the cards ranking from Ace (high) to 2 (low). Ace can also rank low in the sequence A, 2, 3, although the sequence itself ranks high.

Preparation
Minimum and maximum stakes must be agreed beforehand. The maximum should be for each raise, and also for the total to be staked by a player on any one hand. It is recommended that all players begin with an equal bank, and that a game ends when one player loses his entire bank (another game can be started between those who wish to carry on). Otherwise a time should be agreed for stopping, to prevent bad feeling when losers want to carry on to recoup their losses while winners want to get to bed.

All players should deal an equal number of times. It should also be agreed as to whether the cards should be shuffled between deals and, if so, whether it should be a light shuffle or a thorough shuffle. Some prefer to shuffle only when a 'prial' appears. A light shuffle is recommended.

The first dealer can be determined by any acceptable method, and the deal passes to the left after each hand.

Play

The dealer places an 'ante' to the table before him. This is a compulsory bet, usually of the minimum stake. He then deals three cards face down to each player. The remainder of the cards are placed face up to the centre of the table.

Players look at their cards. The object is to hold the best hand after the 'showdown', when the hands are exposed at the end of the deal (see Scoring, below).

The eldest hand (the player to the dealer's left) now has three options: to drop out, by stacking his cards face up on the pile; to 'stay', by putting on the table in front of him a stake equal to the ante; or to 'raise', which is done by putting in a stake equal to the ante, plus another. Thus, if the ante is one unit, he could announce 'stay for one and raise by three', putting in four units in all.

Subsequently all players in their turn must either drop out, stay, in which case they put in a stake equal to the current level of the stake, or raise, as described.

When the turn to bet comes round again to a player who has already bet, that player again has the same options: to drop out; to stay, by adding to his stake enough to bring it to the new level if it has risen since the last bet; or to raise.

A deal can end in one of four ways:

i) all players can drop out except one, who wins and collects the total stake

ii) if two players remain in, either can 'call' the other, by equalizing the stake and announcing 'I'll see you', upon which the player called exposes his hand and wins or loses accordingly (the caller, if the loser, can concede without exposing his own hand if he wishes)

iii) if all players remaining in have equal stakes and have declined the opportunity to raise, in which case they expose their hands

iv) if the total staked by each player has reached the maximum agreed beforehand, when all hands are exposed

When the winner has collected all the stakes on the table, and the final hands have been returned face up to the stack, the next deal takes place.

If no players bet, ie all drop out on the first round, the dealer retrieves his ante and an amount equivalent to the ante from all the other players.

Scoring The classes of hand, in ranking order, and the probability of their being dealt, are shown in the table that follows.

Among the classes of hand, a prial of 3s ranks highest, then Aces down to 2s.

Among running flushes and runs, A, 2, 3 ranks highest, then A, K, Q, followed by K, Q, J down to 4, 3, 2.

Among equal pairs, the unmatched card decides the ranking.

Among flushes and high cards, if the highest card of two or more hands is equal, the next highest decides, if equal the third highest.

There can be ties in all classes except prials.

Classes of hands in Modern Brag, in ranking order

Name	Description	Possible hands	Probability of being dealt
Prial	Three of the same rank (for example 6, 6, 6)	52	0.24%
Running flush	Three in sequence of the same suit (for example ♦ 7, 8, 9)	48	0.22%
Run	Three in sequence (for example 4, 5, 6)	720	3.27%
Flush	Three of the same suit (for example ♥ A, 4, 2)	1,096	4.96%
Pair	Two of the same rank plus another (for example J, J, 3)	3,744	16.94%
High card	None of the above	16,440	74.39%

There is an anomaly in the rankings, since a running flush is slightly less likely to be dealt than the higher ranking prial. That a run ranks higher than a flush, the opposite to the case in Poker, is not an anomaly; the probability of its occurring is different due to the hands being of a different number of cards.

Variants

Blind betting Much interest is added to the version described above when blind betting is allowed. Any player may bet without looking at his cards (which should not even be touched), which entitles him to stake only half of the stake contributed by 'open' players (ie those who look at their hands). If the first player to bet bets blind, then subsequent blind betters must equal the stake in order to stay; an open better must double it to stay. If the first better bets open, then a subsequent blind better cannot bet more than half the stake of the open better. Subsequently, an open better must increase his stake to that of the previous open better to stay, or can raise or drop out by stacking his cards. A blind better who on his turn wishes to continue betting blind must increase his stake to that of the previous blind better, or half that of the previous open better, to stay, or may raise by no more than half the maximum stake agreed before the game. He has another option, however: he may look at his cards. He can then either drop out, or remain in as an open better, in which case he must raise his stake to that of other open betters in order to stay.

There is a showdown when all open betters have equalized their stakes with each other, and all blind betters have done likewise, and all betters have declined in turn the opportunity to raise. Alternatively, the rule described above – that when only two players remain, one can see the other – applies only if both are open players. If one is open and the other blind, there is a rule that 'you cannot see a blind man', so if the blind player is so inclined, he can continue raising and forcing the open player to double his raises until the maximum stake is reached. The rule about not being able to see a blind man can be relaxed if the last two betters are both blind, when it can be permitted that one can see the other.

In all cases, of course, the winner collects all stakes on the table, including those of players who drop out. If all players drop out except a blind player, who thus wins without the need to expose his hand, he is allowed to keep the same hand unexposed, for the next deal, provided his first bet is a blind bet. He is still dealt a hand for the next deal, which is immediately stacked, because superstitious players do not like the sequence of hands to be disturbed.

While Brag players can claim the game allows a modicum of skill insofar as the value of a hand, and its likelihood of winning, must be judged, blind betters eliminate even that, and the game for them becomes a gamble pure and simple.

Wild cards In all forms of Modern Brag, wild cards (ie cards which can represent any card the holder wishes) can be used. Usually, the black 2s are chosen, but some players like all 2s to be wild. The object is to obtain more higher-value hands, but purists would say they cheapen the hands and find them unappealing.

Seven-card Brag Seven-card Brag lacks the progressive betting of Modern Brag, but uses the same classes of hands. Up to seven may play with the standard pack. Each player, including the dealer, antes an agreed stake to the centre of the table. Seven cards are dealt to each player, from which the player makes the two best Brag hands possible, discarding the seventh card face down. When all have completed their hands, each player exposes his better hand, and the holder of the best hand is decided. All players then expose their second hands, and if the best hand is held by the same player, he wins all the stakes. If, however, the two hands are won by different players, nobody wins, the pool of stakes remains on the table, and each player adds a further stake to it. The cards are then shuffled and re-dealt by the player to the left of the dealer. The adding to the pool increases with each round in which it isn't won, until finally a player wins both hands and scoops the lot.

It is not compulsory to make your best hand from the seven cards, and often advisable not to. Suppose a player is dealt the seven cards in the illustration above. The best possible hand is a prial of Jacks, with an excellent chance of winning, but the second hand, a pair of 10s, is unlikely to win. If, on the other hand, the first hand was chosen as ♣Q, J, 10, it would have a reasonable chance of winning, and if it did the second hand of ♥J, 10, 9 is practically certain to win, too, so the second choice of hands would be the more sound.

Nine-card Brag In Nine-card Brag (for which five players is the maximum), each player is dealt nine cards from which he makes three Brag hands. The mechanics of the game are the same as for Seven-card Brag above, ie to win a player must win all three hands, otherwise all players add another stake to the pool and the cards are re-dealt.

Simple Brag A version of Brag played in the UK but hardly noticed in the text books does not involve raising or the convention of a showdown when stakes are equalized. It is a 'freeze-out' game, in the respect that it cannot end until only two players are left in or a limit reached. Before play begins it is best to agree a limit beyond which a single player's stakes on a hand cannot rise. If the limit is reached and all players stakes are equalized, there is a showdown. There is a uniform stake, which is agreed beforehand, and a maximum number of times which a player may stake on one hand – say 20, 40, 100, or whatever.

Each player deals in turn, the deal rotating to the left, with any acceptable method used to decide the first dealer. Three cards are dealt face down to each player, and the remaining cards placed face down to the dealer's left. As players drop out, their cards are added face down to the pile.

Each player puts the standard stake into a pool as an ante, and the eldest hand has the first opportunity to bet. The hands are valued as for the game of Modern Brag above. Each player in turn must either drop out or add the standard stake to the pool, and this continues round the table for as many rounds as is necessary. There is no raising. Every time a player's turn to bet comes round, the player either adds the uniform stake to the pool or drops out. Only when just two players are left in the game may either bring the game to an end by putting in his stake and announcing 'I'll see you', whereupon his opponent shows his hand. If the hand exposed is the better hand, the first player can concede without the need to show his own hand, if he wishes. If the exposed hand is the weaker, then the winning hand must also be exposed to prove it is the better. If the game ends because the staking limit has been reached, all players still playing equalize their stakes and all show their hands, the winner taking the whole pool. If there is a tie the pool is shared among the winners.

Classical Brag Because this is the version of the game played in Great Britain in the 18th century it often takes precedence in books, but it would be hard to find it played nowadays.

The main differences from the game described above lie in the classes of hands and the fact that three wild cards, called 'braggers', are used. The braggers, of equal status, are ♦A, ♣J, ♦9, and they can be used as whatever card the holder wishes. If used as a card of their own rank they cease to be regarded as braggers.

Runs and flushes are not considered as classes of hand, so suits have no significance. There are only three recognized classes, as follows, in ranking order:

Pair-royal   Three cards of the same rank

Pair   Two cards of the same rank with an unmatched card

High card   None of the above

The highest pair-royal (from which derives the word 'prial', used in Modern Brag) is A, A, A and the lowest 2, 2, 2. The highest pair is A, A, the lowest 2, 2.

A natural pair-royal (one without a bragger) beats a pair-royal with one bragger, which beats a pair-royal with two, and a natural pair beats a pair with a bragger.

With equal pairs, the rank of the unmatched card determines precedence. If the high card in high-card hands is equal, the rank of the second card, or if also equal the third, decides precedence.

Between two hands exactly equal, that held by the player nearest the dealer's left wins. The betting and raising are as for Modern Brag.

Three-stake Brag In this variant of Classical Brag, each player places three stakes, of an agreed amount, before him on the table. These stakes are, in effect, the stakes for three separate games to be played with the same hands.

The dealer deals three cards to each player, as usual, but this time the third card is dealt face up. The rank of this card determines the winner of the first stake, the highest face-up card being the winner. For this round, the braggers (♦A, ♣J, ♦9) represent their actual ranks. If two or more players tie with turned-up cards of equal rank, the one nearest the dealer's left wins the stakes (the dealer being regarded as farthest from his left).

The second stake is decided by the game of Brag as described, with the three braggers counting as wild cards. The initial stake put in by each player is regarded as a bet, and beginning with the eldest hand, each player in turn drops out, stays or raises, and so on as usual, the eventual winner taking all the stakes bet for this round.

Players then place their hands face up before them to decide the winner of the third stake. Braggers once again take their natural value. The object is to achieve a total nearest to 31 with the cards, with or without a draw, with Aces counting eleven, court cards ten and other cards their pip value. Each player can see, with all the cards exposed, the total to beat.

Beginning with the eldest hand, each player can draw one or more cards, passed by the dealer, to get his total nearer to 31. If his total goes over 31, he 'busts' and loses. He can stop when he likes. If two or more hands are equal, the player nearest to the dealer's left wins (it follows that if a player reaches 31 exactly he must win). Note that if a player holds an original hand of three Aces, or two Aces with a court card or a 10, he will have a count of 32 or 33. This is not counted as having 'bust', but of being one or two away from 31, and in the final reckoning will equal a hand of 30 or 29 respectively.

American Brag American Brag was very popular in the USA in the 19th century and is a variant of Classical Brag, except that instead of the braggers being ♦A, ♣J and ♦9, all Jacks and all Nines are braggers. All braggers are considered equal. A peculiarity is that a hand which includes braggers is considered better than a hand of the same class with fewer or no braggers. The best hand is therefore a hand of three braggers. The use of eight braggers rather than three makes the appearance of pairs-royal and pairs much more frequent, of course.

Comet

Comet is one of the earliest known games of the Stops family. It was described in 1768 as a 'new game', but is believed to have got its name in 1758 with the reappearance, as predicted, of Halley's Comet. 'Comet' became popular as a brand name for all sorts of products for many years. It can be played for amusement only, when a scorecard is kept for each player over a number of deals, but as a gambling game it is played so that settlement is made after each deal.

Type	A game of the Stops family
Alternative names	Commit
Players	Two; three to five for variants
Special requirements	Two identical packs of cards; chips or cash for stakes

Aim

To get rid of all the cards in your hand by playing them to the table.

Cards

Two identical standard packs of 52 cards are required, from which are removed the Aces. The red cards are then separated from the black cards. A ♦9 is taken from the red pack and swapped with a ♣9 in the black pack. Two 48-card packs are thus formed, a black pack containing a ♦9 and a red pack containing a ♣9. The two packs are used alternately. The odd card in each pack is called the 'comet', and it is used as a wild card. The other cards are ranked from King (high) to 2 (low), and suits are of no significance.

Preparation

The amount of the stake must be agreed. The stake is paid for every pip that the loser holds in his hand when the winner gets rid of all his cards. As this could be a large number (perhaps even 100) the stake should be small. Alternatively, the stake could be paid for every ten pips, or fraction of ten, that the loser holds.

Players cut the pack which is to be first used, and the player cutting the lower card becomes the dealer. Thereafter the deal passes to the left, and the game should continue until each player has dealt an equal number of times.

The dealer shuffles, the non-dealer cuts and the dealer deals 18 cards to each player in bundles of three. The remaining twelve cards are set aside face down and take no further part in the game.

Play

The non-dealer plays any card to the centre of the table, and continues to play cards to it in ascending sequence irrespective of suit, announcing the rank of the cards as he plays them and announcing the number at which he is forced to stop, for example he may say '5, 6, 7, 8, without 9'; instead of 'without 9' he might say 'no 9'. The turn then passes to the dealer who, if he can, continues the sequence. To follow the example he may announce and play, '9, 10, Jack, without Queen'. The turn to play passes back and forth until one player plays all his cards to the table.

If a player on his turn cannot continue the sequence, he says 'Pass', and the turn passes back to his opponent, who then begins a new sequence by playing any card or cards he wishes. A King is always a stop, and the player playing it begins a new sequence with another card or cards.

All cards played by both players are played to one face-up pile in the centre of the table. Neither player during the play may look back to check which cards have already been played.

Players must play if they can, and cannot pass or stop if able to play a card. There is one exception: a player may reserve the comet if that is the only card he can play.

Only one card can be played at a time, except when a player holds all four cards of the same rank, or three 9s, with or without the comet. He can then play them simultaneously if he wishes. For example, he may play and announce '7, four 8s, three 9s, 10, without Jack'.

The comet can be played at any time in a player's turn, and can represent any card that is required by the sequence. If the sequence is at a stop, it represents any card the player wishes. In either case, it always acts as a stop. The player who plays the comet then begins a new sequence, with any card he chooses.

Settlement When a player goes out, ie gets rid of all his cards, he is paid according to the total number of pips of the cards remaining in his opponent's hand, with court cards counting as ten points each. If a player is caught with the comet in his hand when his opponent goes out, his count for all unplayed cards is doubled.

When a player goes out by playing the comet as his last card (not as a 9) he scores double the count of the cards left in his opponent's hand, and if he goes out by playing the comet as his last card, representing a 9, he scores quadruple his opponent's count.

If the non-dealer goes out on his first turn, he scores double the pip count of his opponent's cards (quadruple if his opponent holds comet). However, if the dealer can also go out in one turn, the deal is a tie.

Strategy In the early play, one should try to get rid of duplicated ranks first. As play progresses it is important to remember which ranks constitute stops for the opponent and to try to play up to them. If the opponent looks close to going out, it is wise to try to play high-ranking cards and to beware of being caught with the comet when the opponent goes out.

Variants

Comet for three to five players Comet can be played by up to five players by reducing the number of cards dealt. With three players each receives twelve cards in bundles of three, leaving twelve cards inactive; with four players, each receives ten cards in bundles of two, with eight inactive; with five players, each receives nine cards in bundles of three, with three inactive.

The turn of play passes to the left, and if all pass on a stop round to the player who caused the stop, then that player begins a new sequence.

Settlement is as before, with each player paying the winner according to the number of pips held in his hand, as described above.

Commit Commit is really the same as Comet, the alternative name coming about, it is thought, merely because of a misspelling as long ago as the early 19th century. The game described above is sometimes called Commit in books, but some use the name Commit to describe this variation, for from three to seven players. It is probably a better game than Comet for the purposes of gambling, particularly for four or more players.

Only one pack is required, from which the ♦8 is removed and not used, leaving a 51-card pack. The ♦9 is the comet. Cards rank from King (high) to Ace (low).

Each player puts a stake of one unit into a pool before the deal. Cards are dealt one at a time. With three players, each receives 15 cards, six remaining face down to one side. With four players each receives twelve cards, with five each receives ten cards, with six each receives eight cards and with seven each receives seven cards, thereby leaving between one and three cards dead on each deal.

A difference from Comet is that sequences have to be of the same suit. The eldest hand (the player to the dealer's left) plays first and can play to the centre any card or sequence of cards he wishes, bearing in mind sequences are in suits, so he may say '3, 4 of hearts, missing 5'. Play circulates to the left, so the player to the eldest hand's left either plays the ♥5 or says 'pass', whereupon the next player has the opportunity. If all pass, the player who last played a card begins a new sequence.

The comet also has a different function to that in Comet. The player who holds it may play it at any time on his turn. The player on his left then has the choice of continuing the sequence where it was, or using the comet (♦9) as the beginning of a new sequence and continuing with ♦10. If he can do neither, the opportunity passes to his left. As soon as a player plays a card to follow the comet the sequence is determined and play continues as normal. From then on, it is unnecessary for play to proceed clockwise. As soon as a card is played, the holder of the next in sequence may announce it and play it. It will be quickly clear when a stop is reached, and the player of the last card begins a new one.

Settlement The player of the comet wins two units of the stake from each player. The player of a King wins one unit from each player. The first player to get rid of his cards wins the pool, and also wins an extra unit for each King any player is holding at the end, and two from a player careless enough to be holding comet.

Crazy Eights

Crazy Eights is a simple gambling game unrelated to another game called Crazy Eights which is a version of Switch.

Type	A game of pure chance
Alternative names	None
Players	Two to eight; four to eight is best
Special requirements	Chips or cash for staking; a bowl or saucer to hold a pool of stakes

Aim
To play all your cards to the centre.

Cards
The standard pack of 52 cards is used. The ranking of the cards is immaterial, but for settlement purposes cards have the following points values: Aces 15, court cards 10, other cards their pip value.

Preparation
The value of the stake must be agreed.

Any player may pick up the cards, shuffle and begin to deal cards one at a time to each player round the table until a Jack appears. The player dealt the Jack becomes the first dealer. The deal then rotates clockwise.

Each player puts a stake of two units into the centre to form a pool. The dealer shuffles, the player to his right cuts, and the dealer deals five cards face down to each player, including himself, one at a time. He then lays out the next eight cards face up to the centre in two rows of four, and puts the rest to one side. It doesn't matter if ranks are duplicated.

Play
Beginning with the eldest hand (the player to the dealer's left), each player in turn may lay one card only from his hand face up to a card in the centre matching it in rank. As play progresses, more than one player may play a card to the same card in the centre. A player who cannot match a card in his hand with one in the centre passes.

Settlement Should a player get rid of all his cards, he shouts 'Crazy Eights' and collects the whole pool.

Should the game end without any player being able to get rid of his cards, each player counts the total value of the cards in his hand, based on the scale already given. Half the pool goes to the player with the highest count, and half to the player with the lowest. If two or more share for highest or lowest, their half of the pool is divided between them, with any units over being left in the pool for the next game.

Example game

Player A   Player B   Player C

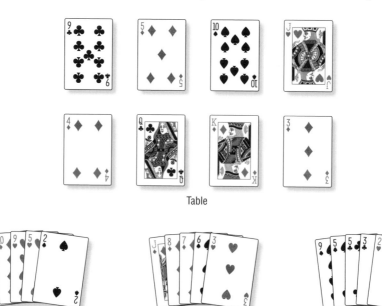

Table

Player D   Player E   Player F

In the illustration, no player managed to scoop the pool of twelve units. The scores were as follows:

Player A	15 (two cards left)
Player B	12 (two cards left)
Player C	23 (four cards left)
Player D	2 (one card left)
Player E	21 (three cards left)
Player F	2 (one card left)

Thus Player C took six units for highest, and Player D and Player F took three units each for joint lowest.

Easy Go

Easy Go is a version of the simple game of Put and Take adapted to playing cards. It is a game of no skill whatever and is a rapid method of redistributing wealth on the basis of luck.

Type	A game of winning or losing on the turn of a card
Alternative names	None
Players	Any number to a maximum of eight
Special requirements	Chips or cash for betting; a bowl or saucer for holding the pool of stakes

Aim
To win as much money as possible. Secondary aim: to lose it gracefully.

Cards
The standard pack of 52 cards is used.

Preparation
One player volunteers to be both banker and dealer. The bank passes round the table clockwise with each deal, the dealer always being also the banker. There is no advantage to being the banker.

The banker shuffles, the player to his right cuts, and the banker deals five cards, one at a time, to each player, except himself. Players display their hands face up on the table before them.

Play
The banker places a card face up before him on the table. A player whose hand includes the card of the same rank and colour places two units of the stake into a pool in the centre of the table, and a player whose hand includes a card of the same rank but opposite colour puts one unit into the pool. A player who holds two or three cards of the same rank has to put units into the pool for each.

The banker then places a second card face up before him. This time a player with the card of the same rank and colour puts in three units, and a player with a card of the same rank and opposite colour two units.

The banker turns up in the same manner three more cards. On the third card the rates for putting into the pool are five units for the same colour, four for the opposite. On the fourth card the rates are nine units and eight units, and on the last 17 units and 16 units.

When all players have finished putting into the pool, the opposite process begins.

The five cards used by the banker are put to one side and the banker deals himself the first of a second batch of five cards face up. This time a player with a card of the same rank and colour takes two units from the pool, and a player with a card of the same rank but opposite colour takes one unit. The same procedure is followed for four more deals, the players taking from the pool the numbers of units corresponding to the numbers they were required to put in on the first five of the banker's cards.

If during the taking-out stage the pool is exhausted, the banker is obliged to put more units in to enable all the players to be paid. On the other hand if, after the taking-out stage, some stakes remain, the banker takes them.

The cards are collected together and handed to the player on the banker's left, who becomes both banker and dealer for the next hand.

Example hand

Five cards each are dealt to five players, Players A to E, as in the illustration opposite.

The banker's five cards for the putting-in stage are shown underneath.

On the first card, Player A and Player D both have a 6 of the opposite colour and put one unit into the pool. On the second card Player B puts in three units and Player E two. At the end of the putting-in phase, Player A has put in one unit, Player B eleven, Player C none, Player D 18 and Player E eleven, a total of 41 units in the pool.

The banker's five cards for the taking-out stage are also shown.

The players took out as follows: Player A eight units, Player B six, Player C 16, Player D two and Player E 18, a total of 50 units.

Overall, Player C won 16 units, and Player A and Player E seven each. Player B lost five units and Player D 16. The banker lost 9 units, having been 24 in profit before his last card, which forced him to add to the pool.

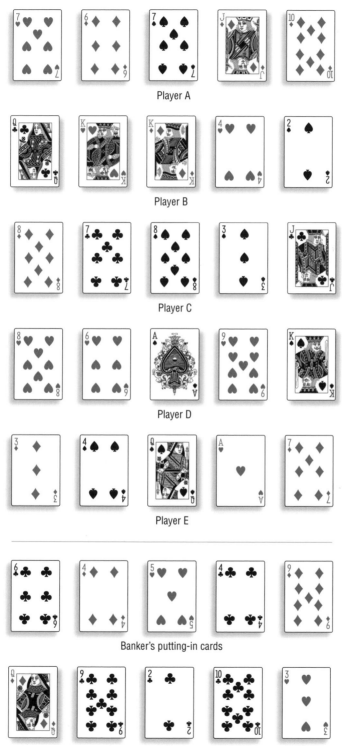

Player A

Player B

Player C

Player D

Player E

Banker's putting-in cards

Banker's taking-out cards

Hoggenheimer

Hoggenheimer is merely an adaptation of the casino gambling game Roulette. Because it was invented in the UK it is sometimes called English Roulette.

Type	A banking game played privately
Alternative names	English Roulette
Players	Any number
Special requirements	Chips or coins for staking

Aim
To win chips by betting on cards in the layout.

Cards
The standard pack of 52 cards is used, from which are removed the 6s, 5s, 4s, 3s and 2s and a Joker added, making a pack of 33 cards. The Joker must be indistinguishable in its condition from the rest of the pack; if it is cleaner from lack of use, then the ♣2, for example, could be used in its place.

Preparation
One player must be a banker. Should there be no volunteers, or if more than one wish to be banker, players draw a card from the pack and highest becomes banker (Ace high, 2 low). The odds later quoted for the game are true, so there is no advantage to holding the bank. A banker may relinquish the bank when he chooses. If there is competition for the bank, it should be agreed that a player holds the bank for a certain number of deals.

The banker has the right to shuffle last, and may ask any player to cut the cards. The banker lays out 32 cards face down in four rows of eight, laying aside for the moment the final card, face down.

The four rows represent the four suits: from the top, spades, hearts, diamonds and clubs. The eight columns represent the ranks: Aces on the left down to 7s on the right.

The players place bets upon whether a certain card, or combination of cards, will be exposed, ie turned face up, at the end of the game. The chips are placed in the same way that they are placed on a Roulette table.

Play
When the bets are placed, the banker turns over the odd card, and places it in its place on the layout, for example the ♠A goes in the top left-hand corner, the ♣7 in the bottom right-hand corner. The card in that place is turned over and put into its place, the card replaced going to its place, and so on. The game ends when the Joker is turned up, at which stage some cards will be exposed and others not. The banker then pays out those who made winning bets and takes for himself all losing bets.

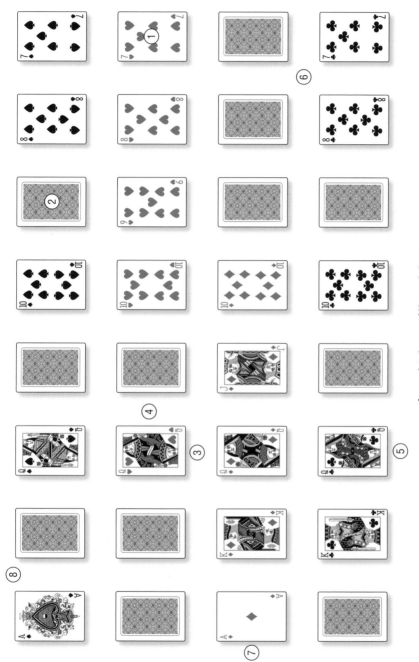

A completed game of Hoggenheimer

An explanation of the various bets, and the odds they pay, is best made by referring to the illustration of a completed game on the previous page. The bets, and odds, are as follows:

On a single card	The stake is placed on the chosen card and the odds paid are evens, or 1–1.
	In the illustration, stake 1 on the ♥7 is successful, stake 2 on ♠9 loses.
On a pair of adjacent cards, either in a row or column	The stake is placed between the two cards. The odds paid are 2–1.
	Stake 3 on the two red Queens has won, stake 4 on the Queen and Jack of hearts has lost.
On any four cards, either in a column or a square	For a column the stake is placed below it, for a square it is placed in the centre. The odds paid are 4–1.
	Stake 5 is placed on the four Queens and has won, stake 6 on the square of ♦8, 7, ♣8, 7 has lost.
On any eight cards, either in a row or in two adjacent columns	The stake is placed either at the end of the row or between and at the end of the two columns. The odds paid are 8–1.
	Stake 7 is on the whole of the diamond suit and stake 8 is on all the Aces and Kings. Both have lost.

So in this particular game, where 20 of the 32 cards were exposed before the Joker appeared, there were eight bets of which three won. If all were of one chip, the banker ended two chips down.

Lansquenet

Lansquenet is mentioned by the French writer Rabelais in his bawdy book *Gargantua* (1534). The game takes its name from the *landsknecht*, mercenary German knights who at the time roamed Europe getting into mischief. They often carried specially made cards, with *landsknechte* representing the Jacks, with which they gambled with the local populace. Their cavalier reputation gave a very simple game a spurious romantic aura, which has ensured its survival, at least in books.

Type	A simple banking game of no skill
Alternative names	None
Players	Two or more
Special requirements	Chips or cash for betting

Aim
To bet on a card that is not 'matched' before the banker's card.

Cards
The standard pack of 52 cards is used.

Preparation
The cards are shuffled by a first and then cut by a second player. Any player then deals a card face up in turn to each player, including himself. The first player to be dealt a Jack becomes the first banker. Thereafter the bank passes to the left for each deal. The game ends by consent when each player has been banker an equal number of times. The banker stipulates the minimum and maximum betting stake.

Play
The banker shuffles the cards and the player to his right cuts. The banker then deals the betting layout. Provided there is no duplication of the ranks, he deals four cards. The first two are dealt side by side and are called 'hand cards', the next is the 'banker's card' and is dealt below the hand cards, and the fourth is the 'players' card' and is dealt above the hand cards (see illustration, p47).

If there are duplications of rank, the procedure is as follows:

a) If the second hand card matches (ie is of the same rank) the first, it is placed on top of the first, and a new card is dealt. This is repeated, if necessary, until the hand cards are of two different ranks.

b) If the banker's card matches a hand card, it is placed on top of the hand card, and this too is repeated if necessary until the banker's card differs in rank to the hand cards.

c) If the players' card matches a hand card, it is handled as per the banker's card. If the players' card matches the banker's card, all cards are collected up, shuffled, and a new layout dealt.

When the layout is complete, with four different ranks shown, players place their stakes by the players' card, taking care to remember which stake is their own. Initially, they have no choice on which card to bet. The hand cards are dead and do not enter the play – they merely remove two ranks from the betting.

The banker then deals the top card from the pack to the table. If it matches one of the hand cards, it is placed on top of the hand card. If it matches in rank the players' card, the banker wins and takes all stakes on the players' card. If it matches the banker's card, the players win, and the banker pays all those who bet on the players' card at even money, ie the players each win the amount of their stake.

If the dealt card does not match any of the four ranks in the layout, it is placed alongside the players' card and becomes a second players' card, and all players may bet on this card as well, within the limits, whether or not they have bet on the first card.

The banker then deals the next card to the table, which might settle all of the bets (if it is the banker's card), some of the bets (if it matches one of the players' cards), or it might provide a further players' card on which all players are entitled to bet.

When a players' card is matched, and the banker has collected the stakes, the dealt card is placed upon the players' card that it matched, and the rank becomes dead, having the same status as the hand cards.

Each time a new players' card is established, all players may bet on it, but they cannot increase or decrease their stakes on other cards, nor may they remove stakes or transfer them to other players' cards. The banker continues to deal cards from the pack until he matches his own card, whereupon he pays all bets on players' cards and his deal ends, the role of banker passing to his left.

Example hand

The illustration opposite shows a game in progress. The first four cards dealt were ♠K, ♠3 (hand cards), ♦4 (banker's card) and ♣J (players' card). Four players staked 12 chips on ♣J. The cards dealt by the banker when play commenced were: ♦7 (a new players' card, on which four players staked ten chips), ♣10 (a third players' card, on which three players staked six chips), ♥K (placed on ♠K as a hand card), ♥J (the banker collected the 12 chips staked on ♣J, and placed ♥J on ♣J, the Jack rank now joining the King rank and 3 rank as dead), and ♠4. The ♠4 matches the banker's card, which ends the game, so the banker now pays out ten chips to those players who bet on ♦7 and six chips to those who bet on ♣10. The banker's turn now ends (he suffered an overall loss of four chips) and the bank passes to the left. In general, there is no advantage or disadvantage to the banker.

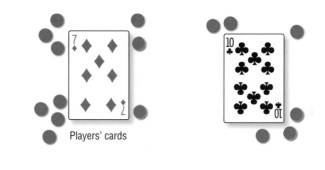

Players' cards

Hand cards

Last card dealt

Banker's cards

Le Truc

Le Truc is an old French gambling game dating back to the 16th century. It is a simple, but not unskilful game, which can entail a degree of bluffing. However, unlike Poker in which bluffing is an essential part, Le Truc is a game which can be played using a points-scoring system, without the betting element. The game described here is a version in which betting is involved and settlement is made after each hand.

Type	A trick-taking game
Alternative names	None
Players	Two
Special requirements	Chips or cash for betting

Aim
To win the majority of tricks, ie two or three.

Cards
The standard pack of 52 cards is used, from which are removed the 8s, 5s, 4s, 3s and 2s, making a pack of 32 cards. The cards rank in the order of 7 (high), 6, Ace, King, Queen, Jack, 10, 9 (low). The suits are of no significance.

Preparation
The basic stake for each game must be agreed (it may be doubled up to six times during a game).

Players cut for first deal, and the player holding the lowest card deals, cards being in their usual order from Ace (high) to 6 (low). Subsequently the deal alternates.

The dealer shuffles, and the non-dealer cuts. The dealer deals three cards to each player, one at a time, beginning with the non-dealer.

The non-dealer studies his hand and has two options. He may say 'I play' in which case the play starts, or he may request a new deal, in which case the dealer may agree or refuse. If he agrees, the hands are laid aside face down and the dealer deals two fresh ones. If the dealer refuses a new deal, the players start with the hands dealt to them.

Play
Suits are immaterial, so there are no trumps and no obligation to follow suit. Players can play whichever cards they like to each trick; see p148 for an explanation of tricks and trick-taking. A trick is won by the higher card it contains. If both players play a card of equal rank, the trick is 'spoiled', and is claimed by the player who won the first trick. If the first trick is spoiled, then it is claimed by the player who wins the second trick, and if both are spoiled, they are claimed by the player who wins

the third. If all three tricks are spoiled, the hand is tied and the deal passes. The leader to a trick which is spoiled leads to the next.

Each deal is worth the basic stake to the winner of the majority of the three tricks, but the attraction of the game (which introduces the possibility of bluffing) is the opportunity to double. A player, before playing a card at any time, whether leading or following to any of the three tricks, may offer to double the value of the hand. His opponent may either decline, in which case he concedes the hand at the value before the offered double, or he accepts. A hand may be doubled a maximum six times, making its value 64 points (1, 2, 4, 8, 16, 32, 64).

A player offers to double by stating the new proposed value for the hand, for example if the hand is worth one, he will say 'two if I play'. His opponent accepts by saying 'yes', and the doubler proceeds to lay his card. The opponent declines by laying aside his hand face down.

Strategy In the question of deciding to play, a player with a poor hand may occasionally offer to play, and even double in the hope of forcing his opponent to throw in his hand. His opponent, of course, must use judgement in accepting or refusing such offers.

In the play, it is generally considered necessary to try to win the first trick, because that ensures one will win the hand if either subsequent trick is spoiled. However, this doesn't always apply. The order in which the player plays his cards can be vital, as the example hand will show.

Example hand
Suppose the hands are as illustrated.

Non-dealer   Dealer

If the non-dealer decides to make certain of not losing the first trick, to ensure he wins the hand if a subsequent trick is spoiled, he will lead ♦7. The play will proceed:

	Non-dealer	*Dealer*
1	♦7	♣K
2	♣A	♠6
3	♥K	♦A

The dealer wins the hand 2–1.

If the non-dealer leads his Ace, the outcome will be the same. The dealer will win the first trick with his 6, and must win another whichever card he leads: if he leads his King he wins the third trick with his Ace. If he leads his Ace at the second trick, he again wins the third trick, which will be spoiled, with his King, by virtue of having won the first.

But suppose the non-dealer leads his King. He is now sure to win the hand, whatever the dealer plays. The likeliest outcome is:

	Non-dealer	Dealer
1	♥K	♦A
2	♦7	♠6
3	♣A	♣K

The non-dealer wins the hand 2–1.

Suppose, however, in the last example, the dealer, after winning the first trick, had doubled? The non-dealer would know that if the dealer holds a 7 the dealer must win. Would he accept the double, or would he refuse it and thus lose a game he must win? Similarly, in the first example, had the non-dealer doubled before leading to the second trick, would the dealer have accepted? He would know that should non-dealer hold another 7 or a 6, non-dealer must win.

Experience is the best teacher in deciding what is a good hand, what to lead and when to double and when to accept a double.

Loo

Loo dates from the 17th century, and for more than 100 years was one of the most popular card games in Britain. It was originally called Lanterloo, from the French *lanterlu*, which has been translated as 'fiddlesticks' and was the chorus of a popular song. It was supplanted in the late 19th century by the similar game of Napoleon. There are three-card and five-card versions, and limited and unlimited versions. The main description here is of three-card limited Loo.

Type	A trick-taking game
Alternative names	None
Players	Three to seventeen; six or seven is best
Special requirements	Chips or cash for staking; a bowl or saucer for holding the pool of stakes

Aim
To win at least one trick in each hand, thus winning chips.

Cards
The standard pack of 52 cards is used, the cards ranking from Ace (high) to 2 (low). For fewer than five players it's preferable to reduce the pack to 32 cards by removing the 6s, 5s, 4s, 3s and 2s, the cards ranking from Ace (high) to 7 (low).

Preparation
A unit of stake should be agreed. For this description it is assumed to be one chip.

Any player may pick up the cards, shuffle and begin to deal cards one at a time to each player round the table until a Jack appears. The player dealt the Jack becomes the first dealer. The deal subsequently passes to the left.

Before each deal, the dealer must put an agreed stake into a pool. It must be divisible by three, as a third of it is taken by the winner of each trick, so the pool should be of three chips. Ideally, the game should not end before each player has been dealer an equal number of times.

The dealer shuffles the cards and the player to his right cuts. Beginning with the 'eldest hand' (the player to the dealer's left), the dealer deals one card at a time clockwise to each player, including himself, and one to an extra hand, called 'miss', until each has three cards. He then places the remaining cards face down in the centre with the top card turned face up. The suit of this card is the trump suit.

Play
The players examine their hands and, beginning with the eldest hand, each has three choices. First, he may play with the hand dealt him. Second, he may exchange his hand for 'miss' and play with that, discarding the hand he was dealt face down.

Third, he may decline to play, in which case he again discards his hand face down. Of course, once a player decides to play with miss, subsequent players have only two choices: to play or to decline.

The player who first decides to play leads to the first trick; see p148 for an explanation of tricks and trick-taking. A trick is won by the highest trump it contains, or the highest card of the suit led if it does not contain a trump.

However, the normal rules of trick-taking do not apply, and Loo's trick-taking rules are quite eccentric:

i) A player must follow suit, if able, and if 'void' (ie if he does not hold any cards in that suit) must trump, if able. In either case, he must 'head' the trick if able, ie play a card to beat the previous highest card in the trick.

ii) If the player leading the trick holds the Ace of trumps (or the King if the Ace was the turn-up) he must lead it.

iii) If the player leading the trick holds two or more trumps he must lead one, and if there are only two players left in the game he must lead the higher or highest of his trumps.

If a player fails to observe these rules and this 'revoke' is not discovered and put right before the next player plays, the hand is abandoned and the pool shared between all those playing except the revoker, any odd chips being left in for the next deal. The revoker must additionally provide six chips for the following pool (ie double the usual number).

When the hand is finished, each player takes one third of the pool for each trick won (which is why the initial pool is of a multiple of three chips). A player who played but failed to win a trick is 'looed'. He must put three chips into the next pool (this is why players may choose not to play – they lose the chance of a share in the pool, but they avoid the risk of having to put in three chips for being looed). The chips put in by looed players form the succeeding pool, and the dealer avoids needing to provide the pool. If no player is looed, the dealer puts in three chips as usual.

If all the players refuse to play on any deal, the dealer takes the pool (he may or may not have provided it himself) and the deal passes. If only one player has chosen to play by the time the choice reaches the dealer, then the dealer must play. He can, however, protect himself from being penalized for being looed by announcing that he will play for the pool instead of for himself. This means any chips he might be entitled to for winning tricks remain in the pool.

Example hand
Suppose five players have chosen to play and there are nine chips in the pool. The hands are as illustrated, with clubs the trump suit.

| Player A | Player B | Player C | Player D | Player E |

Player A is the eldest hand and leads. The play proceeds:

	Player A	Player B	Player C	Player D	Player E
1	♦ K	♦ 5	♥ K	♦ Q	♣ J
2	♣ 5	♣ A	♠ Q	♣ 6	♠ A
3	♦ J	♥ 8	♥ A	♣ 8	♠ 5

Player B, Player D and Player E each collect three chips from the pool, and Player A and Player C must each put three chips in to form a pool of six chips for the next hand.

Variants

Loo has been played for hundreds of years and from time to time minor variations to the above have been popular. The biggest variation is in the number of cards in the hand. The differences between three-card Loo, as described above, and five-card Loo are as follows.

Five-card Loo Each player is dealt five cards. The maximum number of players is therefore ten. The pool must consist of five chips, and a player looed must put five chips into the pool for the following hand.

There is not a miss hand.

A player who has decided to play may exchange any number of cards from his hand with the same number from the top of the stock. He cannot subsequently decide not to play, nor can he exchange before deciding to play. This option is available only while cards remain in stock.

The ♣J is the highest trump no matter what suit is trumps. It is known as 'pam'. The holder of pam must obey the rules which the holder of the Ace faced in three-card Loo, with one exception. If a player leads the trump Ace and announces 'pam be civil', then the holder of pam is barred from playing it on that trick. He must otherwise obey the rules, ie he must play another trump if he holds one.

Should a player hold five cards of the same suit or four plus pam, he has a 'flush' and exposes it, automatically winning the pool, with all other players looed. A player may find he holds a flush after exchanging cards and may declare it then. All other players are looed even if they have already declined to play. The hands are not played out. Should two or more flushes be held in the deal, a flush in the trump suit takes precedence over one in a plain suit. Otherwise the highest card in the suit decides precedence, if equal the second highest and so on. Exactly equal flushes share the pool equally.

Irish Loo This is played as three-card Loo, with two differences. Firstly, there is no miss, but a player who decides to play may exchange any number of cards by discarding and drawing the same number from the stock. Secondly, if clubs are trumps, no player may drop. This leads to more players being looed and consequently bigger pools.

Unlimited Loo All versions of the game described are known as 'limited' games. They can all also be played as 'unlimited' games. 'Limited' refers to the obligation of a player looed to put chips into the pool for the following deal, which in the games above is limited to three chips for three-card Loo and five for five-card Loo.

In unlimited Loo a player who is looed puts into the next pool the amount of the pool at the beginning of the deal. Thus if two players are looed in a game where the pool is nine units, as in the example hand above, they each put nine chips into the next pool, making a pool of 18 chips. If two are looed in this deal, the pool reaches 36 chips. The pool can soon reach such large amounts that only very rich gamblers play unlimited Loo.

Monte Bank

Monte Bank was a popular game in illegal gambling clubs and casinos in many countries of North and South America. It was run by the house which took a percentage of the turnover. A much simpler game was developed from it for private use. As the casino game is more interesting and offers more betting options, a modified form of it is described first, with the simpler private game described as a variant.

Type	A banking game of chance
Alternative names	Spanish Monte
Players	Three or more
Special requirements	Chips or cash for betting; a bowl or saucer to hold the pool of stakes

Aim
To bet on a rank of card which will be 'matched' before other ranks.

Cards
A standard pack from which are removed the 10s, 9s and 8s, leaving a pack of 40 cards.

Preparation
A minimum and maximum bet must be agreed. A first banker must be chosen by spreading the pack, with all those who wish to be banker drawing a card, the player to draw the highest (Ace high, 2 low) becoming first banker. The banker shuffles and the player to his right cuts.

Play
The banker draws two cards from the bottom of the pack and places them face up side by side on the table. This is the bottom layout. If the cards are of the same rank, the second must be put to one side and another dealt from the bottom of the pack. This must be repeated until the cards are of different ranks. He then draws two cards from the top of the pack and lays them face up above the first two. This is the top layout. If either or both matches (ie is of the same rank as) a card in the bottom layout, it must be put to one side and replaced. If the cards match each other, then the second must be put aside and replaced. This must continue until the four cards in the layout are of different ranks.

If no cards have been put aside, the game may commence. If any cards have been put aside, they must now be incorporated into the pack, which the banker reshuffles and passes to the player on his right to cut. This player places the pack face down before the banker. It is essential that the bottom card is not seen by any players.

Play commences with the players placing bets, within the limits for each bet, on a card or combination of cards. They are betting that the rank of the card or one of those in their combination, will be matched in play before the rank of all or some of the other cards. The various bets, and where they are placed, are best described by reference to the illustration.

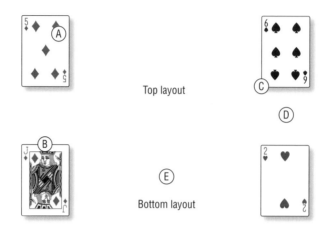

Top layout

Bottom layout

They are:

i) A circle bet. This is a bet on one rank to be matched before any of the other three in the layout. The stake is placed on the card itself. In the illustration, stake A is a bet that a 5 will be turned up before a 6, 2 or Jack. Successful bets are paid at odds of 3 to 1.

ii) A crisscross bet. This is a bet that one rank will be matched before a certain other rank in the layout. The stake is placed on the side of the card facing the card bet against, or, if the card bet against is diagonally opposite the chosen card, on the facing corner. Thus, in the illustration, stake B is a bet that a Jack will be turned up before a 5, stake C is a bet that a 6 will be turned up before a Jack. Successful bets are paid at odds of 1 to 1, or evens.

iii) A doubler bet. This is a bet that one of a pair of ranks in the layout will be matched before one of the remaining two ranks in the layout. The stake is placed between the two ranks bet upon. Thus stake D is a bet that a rank in the right layout (either a 6 or a 2) will be turned up before a rank in the left layout (either a 5 or a Jack), and stake E is a bet that a rank in the bottom layout (a 2 or a Jack) will be turned up before a rank in the top layout (a 5 or a 6).

Players are not confined to a single bet each, and may place more than one bet, provided each bet is within the staking limits.

When all bets are made, the banker turns the pack face up, exposing what was previously the bottom card of the pack. If the rank of this card coincides with the rank of any of the cards in the layout, any bets affected are settled by the banker, and if no other bets concern the card in the layout, it is removed.

Having settled the bets, if any other bets remain on the layout, the banker removes the exposed card to reveal the next card, settling any relevant bets, and so on.

Once all bets are settled, the cards are collected and thoroughly shuffled and the bank passes to the next player to the banker's left. Nobody is compelled to take the bank, and any player may pass it on to the next if he wishes. There is no advantage or disadvantage to holding the bank.

Example game

Suppose, with the layout and betting as illustrated opposite, the cards exposed by the banker are as follows:

i) ♣3. This is of no significance and is discarded.

ii) ♠A. As above.

iii) ♠2. Bets D and E are both winners, D because the right-hand layout has beaten the left, and E because the bottom layout has beaten the top. The players who staked D and E each receive their stake back plus an amount equivalent to their stake as winnings from the banker. The ♥2 can be removed from the layout and discarded as no bets now concern it. Bet A, however, is a loser, since a 5 was not the first of the four ranks in the layout to be exposed. The banker collects stake A, but the ♦5 remains in the layout, since stake B involves the 5, being a bet that a Jack will be exposed before a 5.

iv) ♦Q. As (i) and (ii) above.

v) ♣2. As the rank of 2 is not now involved, this is discarded.

vi) ♠5. The banker now removes stake B, as this was a bet that a Jack would be exposed before a 5. The ♦5 can now be removed from the layout and discarded, but ♦J remains as stake C depends upon it.

vii) ♠K. As (i) and (ii) above.

viii) ♦6. Stake C is a winner, as a 6 was exposed before a Jack. Stake C is returned to its owner with an equivalent sum as winnings.

No more bets remain on the layout for settlement, so the hand is at an end and the bank passes. Of the five bets made, the banker won two: A and B, and lost three: C, D and E.

Variant

The more usual private game is simpler, with a choice of only two bets, and only one card exposed by the banker. A big difference from the game described above is that it is the suit, not the rank, which must be matched for a winning bet.

The cards required (ie the 40-card pack) and the preparation are as described above.

Play

The banker draws the bottom two cards from the pack and lays them face up on the table side by side. This is the bottom layout. He then draws the top two cards from the pack and lays them face up above the other two. This is the top layout. The layouts remain as dealt. It does not matter if a suit or a rank is duplicated. The pack is placed face down on the table. No one at any stage should be able to see the bottom card.

The players bet on whichever layout they choose. This is their only choice. The banker then turns over the whole pack, exposing what was the bottom card, which is known as the 'gate'.

If either layout shows a card of the suit of the gate, then those who backed that layout are paid out at even money, or 1–1, ie they receive the amount of their stake plus their stake back. If both cards of a layout are the same as the gate, backers of that layout are paid at 3–1, ie they win three times the amount of their stake and receive their stake back.

Players who bet on a layout which does not include the suit of the gate lose.

There is a slight advantage to the banker if the layouts contain two or more cards of the same suit. For example, suppose in the illustration that follows under Example game that the spade in the bottom layout had been a club, making two clubs in the layouts. There would then be only eleven clubs in the pack, making the odds of a club being the gate 37–11 against, and the overall chance of a bet on either layout winning 25–23 against. The banker would win both bets on 13 occasions (when a spade was the gate), lose both on eleven (a club) and win one and lose one on 24 (a diamond or a heart). If there is one card of each suit in the two layouts, then the game is fair to both sides. It follows that players hoping not to lose money would be advised to bet only on a layout that did not duplicate a suit from the other layout.

It would be a better game, in fact, and the suggestion is put forward, that the two layouts should be dealt face down. Players make their bets, the gate is revealed, and only then are cards in the two layouts exposed and settlement made.

Example game
In the illustration, the pack was turned over to reveal ♥A as the gate.

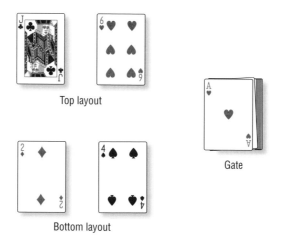

Top layout

Gate

Bottom layout

The backers of the top layout therefore won, as it included ♥6. The backers of the bottom layout, which did not include any hearts, lost.

Napoleon

Napoleon (or Nap, as it is almost always known), is the British representative of the many five-card trick-taking games, the earliest known of which is Triomphe which was played in the 17th century. Games of the same type which became popular in other parts of the world are Euchre, Écarté and Spoil Five.

The name Napoleon was not given to the game until the late 19th century, and it is therefore not thought to be linked to the most famous Napoleon, although the later introduction of bids called 'wellington' and 'blücher' have established a link.

Type	A trick-taking game
Alternative names	Nap
Players	Two to eight; five is perhaps best
Special requirements	Chips or cash for staking

Aim
To win a contract to make a certain number of tricks, and then fulfil that contract in the play.

Cards
The standard pack of 52 cards is used, the cards ranking from Ace (high) to 2 (low).

Preparation
Players draw cards from a spread pack to determine the first dealer. The drawer of the lowest card deals. A peculiarity is that Ace counts low for this purpose only. The deal subsequently passes to the left with each hand.

The dealer deals five cards face down to each player, one at a time, clockwise to his left.

Bidding Each player, beginning with the 'eldest hand' (the player on the dealer's left) has one opportunity to bid or pass. A bid is an offer to make a stated number of tricks with the trump suit of the bidder's choice. The bidder states only the number of tricks, and does not reveal the intended trump suit. The lowest bid is two, except if all the players pass, leaving only the dealer, he must bid at least one.

Each successive bid must be higher than a previous bid.

A bid to win all five possible tricks is called 'napoleon' or 'nap', and the bidder usually says 'nap'. A further bid is allowed, which is 'wellington'. It, too, is a bid to make all five tricks, but it can be called only after a previous player has bid nap.

Play

The highest bidder, called the 'declarer', leads to the first trick; see p148 for an explanation of tricks and trick-taking. He does not need to name trumps, because the first card led indicates the trump suit. The usual rules of trick-taking apply: players must follow suit to the card led and, if unable, may trump or discard. A trick is won by the highest trump it contains, or if it does not contain a trump, by the highest card of the suit led.

The object of the declarer is to win enough tricks to make the contract, and of his opponents to prevent him. There is no bonus for making tricks in excess of the contract, and once the contract is made it is usual not to play out remaining tricks (but the declarer should show the remaining cards in his hand to prove he has not 'revoked').

Settlement Settlement is made after each hand. A declarer successful in making his contract is paid by each opponent the number of chips corresponding to the number of the bid. If the declarer fails, he pays each opponent the same amount.

There are two exceptions. A successful bid of nap earns ten chips from each opponent, but failure costs only five chips to each. A successful bid of wellington earns ten chips from each if successful, and failure also loses ten chips to each.

Strategy Players should appreciate how many cards are 'sleeping' (ie not in play). With up to five players, there are more cards sleeping than in play, so if a player holds a King, it is more likely than not to be the 'master' (ie the highest card in the suit), as the Ace has more chance to be sleeping than 'active'. So bidding includes an element of working out probabilities. The fewer the players, the more luck enters the game.

However, no matter how many players there are, each one will have a hand that includes a suit of at least two cards. So, holding Ace and a small trump is a long way from guaranteeing two tricks in trumps.

Similarly, even holding three high trumps including the Ace plus a 'side suit' with an Ace and a small card is no guarantee that, having forced out all opposing trumps and won the Ace, the small side-suit card will make the fifth trick and ensure success if bidding 'nap'. This is because opponents discarding on the three trumps will note the discards of the other players, and each will attempt to keep a 'guarded' high card in a suit that the others are discarding, purposely to defeat a declarer trying to make two tricks in the same suit at the end. When trying to defeat a contract, a guarded King, for example, is usually a better combination to keep for the last two tricks than a pair of Kings. If fellow defenders take the same line, and keep two cards of the same suit, then the declarer is unlikely to win the last two tricks with Ace and another by expecting the Ace to make all opponents void in the suit.

Example hand

Five hands are dealt to five players as shown.

Player A   Player B   Player C

Player D   Player E

Player A is the eldest hand and bids first. He passes. Player B bids two. With spades as trumps he will make ♠A, could expect to make ♠10 by trumping a club, and if not will hope ♥Q is the master. Player C bids three on the strength of expecting to make at least two club tricks as trumps and the ♥A. Player D bids four, with ♦A, K certainties. He plans to keep back ♦K to trump in and make his third club on the last trick. Player E passes. Player D is therefore the declarer and leads to the first trick. The play goes as follows:

	Player A	Player B	Player C	Player D	Player E
1	♦6	♦4	♣9	♦A	♦Q
2	♣3	♠10	♣J	♣A	♣5
3	♥5	♥3	♣Q	♣2	♠2
4	♦7	♥Q	♥A	♦K	♠8
5	♦10	♠A	♥4	♣7	♠J

So Player D went down. It was a very optimistic bid. Even without Player A's trumps, Player C could have foiled him by not discarding ♣9 on the first trick. Player A did well not to trump on trick 3, but would have foiled the contract anyway – he had a trump to spare. Had Player D, the declarer, led his King of trumps at trick 2 and ♣A at trick 3, he would still have lost, as Player A would have trumped at trick 4 and led a heart at trick 5.

Had Player B been allowed originally to buy the contract with his bid of two, he would have failed as well, because of Player E's three spades. Had Player C been allowed the contract with his bid of three, he, too, would have failed. Player D ends by paying his four rivals four chips each.

Variants

Bidding Some players allow two additional bids. 'Blücher' is a bid to win all five tricks, and can only be bid if a previous bidder has bid wellington. It is very rare. The contractor receives ten chips from each player if successful (as for napoleon and wellington), but pays out 20 to each if he loses. The other bid is '*misère*'. This is a bid to lose all the tricks, without a trump suit (although some players treat the opening lead as a trump indicator as usual). The bid ranks between three and four, and is worth three chips to or from each player.

Short pack Some players like to shorten the pack to suit the number of players, thereby increasing the skill factor as, with fewer sleeping cards, chance plays a smaller part. This is done by stripping the pack of the smaller denomination cards. Thus for four players the lowest cards might be the 9s, for five players the 7s, for six players the 6s and for seven players the 5s.

Newmarket

Newmarket is a mild gambling game, the modern version of Pope Joan. It takes its name from the famous racecourse, but there are many other names for it and, wherever it is played, there are likely to be minor deviations from the description below. As a gambling game it is more popularly played among families for pennies than among serious gamblers.

Type	A game of the Stops family
Alternative names	Boodle, Chicago, Michigan, Saratoga, Stops
Players	Three to eight
Special requirements	Four cards from another pack; chips or cash for staking; a bowl or saucer to hold the pool of stakes

Aim
To make money by getting rid of your cards, thus winning the kitty, and also to play one or more of the 'boodle' cards, thus winning the stakes placed upon them.

Cards
The standard pack of 52 cards is used, the cards ranking from King (high) to Ace (low). Four cards from another pack are also required; a King, a Queen, a Jack and a 10, each of a different suit.

Preparation
A unit of stake must be agreed. For this description we will assume it is one chip.

The four cards from the other pack (called 'boodle' cards) are laid out in a row upon the table, with a bowl beside them to hold the chips contributed to a kitty.

Any player may pick up the cards, shuffle and begin to deal cards one at a time to each player round the table until a Jack appears. The player dealt the Jack becomes the first dealer. The deal subsequently passes to the left.

Before the deal, each player must place five chips to the centre. One goes into the kitty, and the other four are distributed among the boodle cards as the player wishes; he may place one on each card, all four on one card, or distribute his stake in any other combination.

The illustration overleaf shows a layout as it might be with five players, before the deal.

The dealer then deals the cards one at a time face down to each player and one to a spare or 'dead' hand, which is not used. It does not matter if some players receive a card more than others, as the deal rotates.

Boodle Cards

Kitty

Play

The 'eldest hand' (the player to the dealer's left) plays face up to the table in front of him a card of whichever suit he prefers, but it must be the lowest card he holds in that suit. He announces its rank and suit. The player who holds the next higher card in that suit then plays it face up to the table in front of him and announces it in the same manner, and so on. The playing of the cards is 'stopped' either by the sequence reaching the King, or by it reaching one of the cards in the dead hand. When the sequence is stopped, the player who played the last card begins a new sequence. Like the opening leader, he may lay a card of any suit, but it must be the lowest card he holds in that suit. It may be of the same suit as was stopped, if he wishes, in which case the sequence may also be stopped by reaching the point at which the previous sequence in that suit began.

When a player lays a card matching one of the boodle cards, ie the identical card in both suit and rank, he collects the chips on that card. The first player to get rid of all his cards collects the kitty and play ends. Should any chips be left on the boodle cards, they remain there for the next deal. All players distribute five chips again as before, and the previous eldest hand becomes the dealer for the next hand.

Variants

Michigan Michigan is the most popular name for the game in the USA, where the standard version varies from that described above in the following respects:

Boodle cards	These are A, K, Q, J of different suits (ie Ace is included, not 10).
Rank of cards	The cards rank from Ace (high) to 2 (low).
Staking	The dealer places two chips on each boodle card, while the other players put one (ie there is no choice and the boodle cards are evenly staked). There is no kitty.

Dead hand   The cards are dealt as in Newmarket, except that cards to the spare or dead hand are dealt first rather than last, ie the dead hand is between the dealer and the eldest hand. Moreover, it is not dead, but a 'widow', which belongs to the dealer. After looking at his hand, the dealer may, if he wishes, exchange it with the widow. He is not allowed to look at the widow first, nor is he allowed to change back if he decides he prefers his original hand to the widow. Some players agree that, if the dealer is happy with his dealt hand, another player may buy the widow. Whoever offers most for it, takes it and pays the dealer for it. He may not change his mind after buying it. The original hand of the player who takes the widow is discarded face down and becomes the dead hand.

Stopped suits   When a suit is stopped, the player whose card stopped it must change the suit to restart play, ie he cannot begin a new sequence in the suit that was stopped. Some players restrict this even further, and the new suit must be of the opposite colour to the stopped suit. In either case, if the player due to start the new sequence does not hold a card with which he may legitimately do so, the player on his left begins the new sequence, subject to the same restrictions.

Kitty   In the absence of a kitty, the player who goes out collects one chip from all the other players for each card still held in their hands at the end of the play.

General   Although Newmarket and Michigan are basically the same game, the number of variants listed are numerous. However, neither game is always played as stated, and many players play the game with elements of one and elements of the other. It is not a question of which rules are correct, but of which the players choose to apply. All should agree before play starts, of course.

Ombre

Ombre is an old Spanish game which dates back to the 14th century, and which was very popular in Europe for some 400 years until finally almost extinguished by Whist. It was introduced to England in the late 17th century by Catharine of Braganza, who married Charles II. Versions of it may still be found in Spain and Latin America, and in the USA a simplified form for four players is known as Solo (not to be confused with Solo Whist).

The simplest form of the three-handed game, with its complex ranking of the cards, is described here for those who wish to experience a game of a more leisurely (at least among the aristocracy) age. It is actually a good game.

Type	A trick-taking game
Alternative names	Hombre, Rocamber, Tresillo
Players	Three
Special requirements	Chips or cash for staking; a bowl or saucer for holding the pool of stakes

Aim
If playing as 'ombre', to win more tricks than each of your opponents; if opposing ombre, to win more tricks than ombre or to help the other player opposing ombre to win more tricks than ombre.

Cards
The standard pack of 52 cards is used, from which are removed the 10s, 9s and 8s, leaving a short pack of 40 cards equivalent to the Spanish pack.

In 'plain' (non-trump) suits, the cards rank in different orders according to whether they are red or black. In red suits they rank, unusually, as K, Q, J, A, 2, 3, 4, 5, 6, 7. In black suits they rank normally, ie A, K, Q, J, 7, 6, 5, 4, 3, 2.

In red trump suits the cards rank ♠A (*spadille*), 7 (*manille*), ♣A (*basto*), A (*punto*), K, Q, J, 2, 3, 4, 5, 6. In black trump suits, the cards rank ♠A (*spadille*), 2 (*manille*), ♣A (*basto*), K, Q, J, 7, 6, 5, 4, 3. The three top trumps – spadille, manille and basto – are called the 'matadors'. Hence, when a red suit is trumps, there are twelve trumps (including ♠A and ♣A) and when a black suit is trumps there are only eleven trumps.

Preparation
In Spanish games the normal direction of play is anti-clockwise. Any player takes the pack and deals a card face up anti-clockwise to each player, beginning with the 'eldest hand' (in this case the player to the dealer's right), until a black Ace appears.

The black Ace indicates the dealer. Each deal is a game in itself, and the dealer is decided in the same way.

Each player puts an agreed stake into a pool.

The dealer shuffles and the player to his left cuts. The dealer deals each player nine cards, in three bundles of three, in an anti-clockwise direction. The remaining 13 cards are placed face down in the centre of the table.

Bidding The bidding is to determine 'ombre'. Ombre has the right to name the trump suit and to exchange cards by discarding and drawing from the stock. There is one round of bidding.

The eldest hand (remember, this is the player to the dealer's right) has the first choice to be ombre. A player announces his willingness to be ombre by saying 'I play'. Otherwise he says 'I pass'. If only one player says 'I play', he becomes ombre. A player who says 'I play' might, however, be overcalled by a subsequent player saying 'I play'. The second player is announcing that he is willing to be ombre without exchanging any cards with the stock. The first player who called still has the option to become ombre, but he must state that he also is prepared to play without exchanging any cards. If so, he has precedence over the second bidder.

If all three players pass, the deal is abandoned, and a further deal is made, with the new dealer being decided as above, and the pool remaining where it is for the new deal.

Play
Ombre announces the trump suit. If ombre was unopposed (ie he has the right to exchange cards), he discards as many cards as he wishes, and places them face down to one side. He then draws from the top of the stock the same number, so that his hand remains at nine cards. The player to his right then has the opportunity to change cards, and finally the third player may do so. If there are any cards remaining the third player has the right to decide whether they shall be shown to all players or remain face down. If ombre did not exchange, then the other players do not either.

When the final hands are determined, ombre leads to the first trick; see p148 for an explanation of tricks and trick-taking. The normal rules of trick-taking apply (with one exception, mentioned later). Players must follow suit to the card led and, if unable, may trump or discard as they wish. The trick is won by the highest trump it contains, or if it doesn't contain a trump, by the highest card in the suit led.

The exception to the need to follow suit concerns matadors. If a non-matador trump is led, a player holding only matadors in the trump suit need not follow suit, but can 'renege', ie discard from a non-trump suit. However, if the lead itself is a matador, he must follow suit even if it means playing a lower matador, but he is not forced to beat the lead with a higher matador, so that if he holds only higher matadors, he can renege. The simple effect is that matadors cannot be forced out by the lead of lower trumps, but must be played (if no lower trumps are held) if a higher matador is led.

The winner of a trick leads to the next. The object of each player is to win the most tricks, but a secondary object of the two players opposing ombre, as the settlement details below will make clear, is to attempt to prevent ombre from making the most tricks. It might pay for a player opposing ombre not to win a trick in which the other player opposing ombre has already played a higher card than ombre. This could diminish ombre's chances of winning the most tricks.

Settlement To win, ombre does not need to take the majority of the tricks, but only to take more than either of his opponents (ie four tricks will be sufficient if his opponents split the others 3–2). If ombre wins the most tricks, he takes the pool. This is called *sacardo*.

If one of his opponents wins more tricks than ombre, then ombre pays that player a sum equal to the amount in the pool and the pool remains for the next deal. This is called *codille*.

If one or both of his opponents wins the same number of tricks as ombre, ombre doubles the amount in the pool and the doubled pool is carried forward to the next deal. This is called *puesta*.

It follows that an opponent who can win only one or two tricks should concentrate on trying to win tricks which would otherwise be won by ombre, rather than tricks which the other partner opposing ombre might win.

Example hand
The cards are dealt as illustrated, using the Bridge convention of calling the players North, East and West (South not being used as this is a three-player game).

North

West

East

North was the dealer, so West is the eldest hand. West can see that with clubs as trumps, he will hold three of the top four, so is certain of two tricks, and has a good chance, by exchanging his other six cards, of raising this to four or five, so he says 'I play'. If another player says 'I play' he will back down, since his hand is much too poor as it stands for him to be ombre. As it happens, neither East nor North have good hands, so West is allowed to be ombre.

West discards his six non-trump cards, and picks up two small trumps and the master King of diamonds – not bad, and he probably thinks his chances are at least even.

East, who suspects trumps will be black, decides to ditch his two smallest diamonds. His hand is so poor that he wants to leave North as many cards as possible to exchange, in the hope that he may stop ombre. As it happens, he picks up spadille and the ♦A, thus depriving North of spadille, which he would have liked.

North, who thinks diamonds is much the likeliest trump suit, decides to discard all his spades and the ♥3, which was a good choice – if there had been more cards in the stock, he would have discarded some clubs, too. So the exchange was just about even in its fortunes.

The new hands are shown below, arranged with the trumps to the left of each hand.

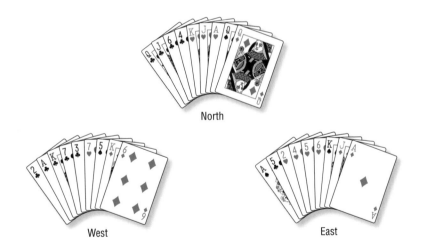

North

West

East

West leads manille. He expects to win four trumps and the ♦K which will be sufficient to score sacardo. East decides to take the trick with spadille (although if he held it back, West would not be able to force it out by leading trumps again). East leads his master spade and then hearts, hoping that North might eventually be able to trump them.

The play goes as follows:

	West (ombre)	East	North
1	♣2 (manille)	♠A (spadille)	♣4
2	♠5	♠K	♠Q
3	♥7	♥6	♥K
4	♣7	♥5	♥J
5	♣A (basto)	♣5	♣6
6	♣K	♥2	♣J
7	♣3	♥4	♣Q
8	♦6	♦A	♥A
9	♦K	♦J	♦Q

West, in the end, was lucky. After losing the first three tricks and then his long trump, he was lucky that North had ♦Q to lead on the last trick. So West takes the pool as sacardo.

Readers might like to work out what might have happened if East had held back spadille on the opening lead.

Panguingue

Panguingue is a game which uses a lot of cards – 320 is about average – and is popular in the south-west of the USA, in Nevada and along the Pacific coast, where there are casinos devoted to it.

It is a game of the Rummy family, descended from Conquian or Coon Can, and is of Spanish origin.

Type	A melding game
Alternative names	Pan
Players	Up to 15; six to eight is best
Special requirements	Eight packs of cards; chips or cash for staking

Aim
To meld all your cards and thus go out.

Cards
Eight standard packs of 52 cards are usually used, but sometimes as few as five or as many as twelve are used. From the packs are traditionally stripped the 10s, 9s and 8s, but as sequences are a vital part of the game, it is logical to strip the Kings, Queens and Jacks instead, which avoids the awkwardness of sequences of 6, 7, J. The amalgamated pack is therefore of 320 cards.

With the court cards stripped, the ranking of the cards is 10 (high) to Ace (low). The following description assumes that the cards used are the 10s down to Aces.

Preparation
The value of the stake should be agreed. In this description it is one chip.

All players shuffle part of the pack, and the pack is then brought together again. Each player draws a card to determine the dealer and the 'eldest hand': the drawer of the lowest card becomes the eldest hand, and the second lowest the dealer. The dealer sits on the eldest hand's left. This is contrary to usual practice in Britain and North America, but it conforms to Spanish tradition where the play is anti-clockwise.

On following deals, the deal does not rotate, either to right or left. The winner of a hand becomes the eldest hand for the next, so the next dealer is the player sitting to the left of the winner. The player to the left of the dealer has the final shuffle. Rarely do all the cards get used during one hand, and between hands it is customary to shuffle only the cards used, together with part of those not used, these then being put at the bottom of the total pack.

Play

The dealer takes roughly as many cards in his hand as will be needed to deal ten cards to each player, with a few over. The cards are dealt anti-clockwise in two bundles of five. The remaining cards are added to the others and are placed face down in the centre to form the 'stock'. It is customary to divide the stock in two, the upper part, called the 'head', being used, while the lower part, the 'foot', is put to one side in case of need.

The top card of the stock is turned face up and placed to the side of the stock to be the 'upcard', which, as other cards are placed on it, becomes a 'discard pile'.

Beginning with the eldest hand, each player in turn to the right of the dealer, after looking at his hand, announces whether he will play or drop out. If he drops out, he must put two chips into a pool. These chips are placed on the part of the stock called the foot, the player who drops out saying he is 'going on top'. He places his cards face down at right angles to the foot. They are not used in the play.

The players who stay in, again in an anti-clockwise direction beginning with the eldest hand, draw a card either from the discard pile or from the top of the stock. To draw from the discard pile requires that the card taken is immediately melded. A meld is usually called a 'spread', and it consists of exactly three cards. There are two kinds: a 'group' and a 'sequence'.

A group is a spread of three cards of the same rank, but there are restrictions in some cases. There are no restrictions to a group of 10s or Aces; they can be made up of any suits. However, for other ranks they must either all be of the same suit, or each of a different suit.

A sequence is usually called a 'stringer', and it consists of three cards of the same suit in sequence.

To meld, a player on his turn lays down before him the three cards of the meld. He may have drawn from the discard pile (in which case, as stated, he must use the card drawn in his meld), or he may have drawn a card from the stock which allows him to meld, or he may have been dealt with a meld.

On his turn, a player may 'lay off' onto his own melds, ie he may add a card or cards to his existing meld or melds. To lay off to a sequence he adds additional cards to the sequence. A group of the same suit may be added to by laying off another card of the same rank and suit. A group of different suits may be added to by laying off cards of any suit (otherwise the group would be limited to four cards, which it is not). Groups of 10s and Aces can also be added to without restriction.

A player can take the top card of the discard pile to lay it off to one of his melds, if he wishes. If he doesn't wish to, he can be forced to lay it off by any other player who demands he do so. This is often done in practice, as it could disrupt a player's hand, especially if he is near to going out, as will be seen later.

Conditions A player who makes certain melds called 'conditions' immediately collects chips from the other active players according to the meld's value. So far as conditions are concerned, certain ranks of cards are known as '*valle* cards' (ie value cards). The valle cards are 7s, 5s and 3s; the other ranks are 'non-valle' cards.

The five classes of conditions melds, and their appropriate payments from each player, are shown in the table that follows.

Three valle cards of different suits	one chip
Three valle cards of the same suit	four chips in spades, otherwise two chips
Three non-valle cards of the same suit	two chips in spades, otherwise one chip
Low sequence (Ace, 2, 3)	two chips in spades, otherwise one chip
High sequence (10, 9. 8)	two chips in spades, otherwise one chip

A player who lays off on a condition, collects the same amount again from each active player, except in the second case above (three valle cards of the same suit), when he collects two chips in spades and one in other suits.

Splitting If a player lays off onto a meld, he may later split off cards from it to make another meld, provided he leaves a value meld. For example, if his original meld was a sequence of ♥ 5, 4, 3, he can on subsequent turns add, say, ♥6 and ♥2. If, on a later turn, he acquires ♥A, he may add ♥A and split the meld into two, ♥ 6, 5, 4 and ♥ A, 2, 3. In this example, he has created a condition (low sequence) and he collects one chip from each player for it. Later, if he added ♥7 to his ♥ 6, 5, 4 sequence he could 'borrow' the ♥4 (because it leaves a valid sequence of ♥ 7, 6, 5) and add the ♥4 to his condition and collect a chip from each player again.

Going out A player's turn consists of drawing a card (either from the discard pile or the stock), melding and/or laying off if he is able to and wishes to (it is not compulsory) and discarding. Throughout the game until the end, therefore, his hand, including cards in hand and those melded on the table, consists of ten cards.

However, when going out, a player is not allowed to discard, and must therefore have eleven cards melded on the table.

A player with three melds on the table and one card in his hand therefore needs to find two cards to lay off. He might pick up from stock a card which he can lay off, but when he discards he will still not have eleven cards melded, so cannot go out, even though he has no cards in his hand. He must continue to draw on his turn until he draws a card he can lay off, in which case he can legitimately go out. (This is where it could be profitable to force a player to take a discard and lay off with it, if it reduces his hand to one card.)

If a player is in the situation where he is waiting for a card to lay off, with ten cards melded, the player to his left must not discard any card which allows him to take it and go out, unless he has no safe card which will prevent it.

If both halves of the stock (head and foot) are exhausted before a player has gone out (a very rare occurrence), the discard pile is turned over and play continues.

Settlement The player who goes out wins the game and collects one chip from each active player (an optional rule stipulates two chips from any player who has not melded), plus the values of any conditions he has (thereby being paid for them twice, as he has already collected once for them during play). He also collects the chips stacked on the foot of the stock from those players who dropped out.

Strategy The initial decision is whether to play or pay two chips to drop out. Because the topmost card of the discard pile cannot be taken without melding, it is difficult to build a hand; one can improve it only by the draws from the stock. Therefore a hand with several unconnected cards in it should be discarded. The hand illustrated is a hand in point.

There are two pairs and six cards which bear very little relation to each other. The prospects of melding conditions or going out are so remote that this hand should be ditched.

On the other hand, the hand illustrated below is ripe with possibilities.

There are two cards towards several melds: a condition of three valle cards of the same suit, conditions of low sequence and high sequence in diamonds; other sequences in clubs and diamonds; and pairs of 8s, 6s and 3s. There is not an unmatched card and excellent prospects of going out. With a hand like this, with a number of cards which can be melded in two different ways, it would be a mistake to lay down melds too early. The cards held in the hand when an opponent goes out are not penalty cards. Of course, a condition should be laid down, and the chips collected for it, because they would be forfeited if an opponent went out.

Pinochle

Pinochle is derived from Bezique, and is practically the same game; Pinochle is the version which took hold in the USA in the late 19th century and became one of that country's most popular games. It is thought that it gets its name from the French and German word *binocle*, meaning pince-nez (*besicles* in French also means 'eye-glasses'). Binocle was an early name for Pinochle and even now nobody can explain the intrusive 'h' in its name; some experts still ignore it and spell the game Pinocle.

The game which took hold in the USA is technically Auction Pinochle with Widow, which is a game for three players and the version of Pinochle most suitable for gambling.

Type	A game which combines trick-taking and melding
Alternative names	None
Players	Three; four, five or six for variants
Special requirements	Two packs of cards; chips or cash for staking, pen and paper for scoring

Aim
To score points by melding and by winning in tricks cards with certain scoring values.

Cards
Two standard packs of 52 cards, shuffled together, are used, from which are removed the 8s, 7s, 6s, 5s, 4s, 3s and 2s, leaving a combined pack of 48 cards. The cards rank Ace (high), 10, King, Queen, Jack, 9 (low).

Preparation
The stake value should be agreed, ie the value of one chip.

Each player cuts, and shows the bottom card of the portion he cut. With the cards ranking as above, the player who draws the lowest card chooses where to sit and becomes the first dealer, with the next lowest sitting to his left. The deal subsequently passes to the left.

The dealer shuffles the pack, and the player to his right cuts. The dealer deals a bundle of three cards, face down, to each of the players clockwise, then three more face down to the centre to form a 'widow'. He then continues to deal to the players four more rounds of cards in bundles of three, so that each player has 15 cards and the widow three.

Bidding Each player in turn, beginning with the 'eldest hand' (the player to the dealer's left), has an opportunity to bid, which is an offer to make a certain number of points. He does not name the trump suit. He may bid or pass, but if he passes he cannot re-enter the bidding later. Bids are expressed in multiples of ten points, and the lowest bid is of 300. Each bid must be higher than the last. The bidding is continuous and ends when two players have passed, the third player who remains becoming the 'bidder'. The bidder will play against the other two players combined, who are the 'opponents', with the object of making the number of points of his bid. If all three players pass, the deal is abandoned, and the deal passes to the left.

Widow When the bidding has finished, the bidder turns over the three cards in the widow so that the opponents can see what they are. He then takes them into his hand.

Melding Only the bidder melds. He announces his melds and then scores for them, and the scores are noted. It is not in the rules for the bidder to be obliged to show his melds, but he must if an opponent asks him to, and in practice it is customary, and common sense, for the bidder to show them. He may change his melds any time before he leads to the first trick.

Burying After melding, the bidder lays away face down any three cards that he has not used in a meld (which makes it sensible that he should lay his melds on the table, so that the opponents can see that the buried cards were not used in melds). This is called 'burying', and it brings his hand back to 15 cards. At the same time, he announces the trump suit. He is not obliged to state whether or not he has laid away a trump. He is permitted to change his mind about the trump suit and the cards he is burying (as well as his melds) any time before he makes the first lead. When the bidder has decided on the trump suit and his melds, it is customary, rather than to note the points of his melds, to note the points he needs in play to make his bid. For example, if he has bid 350, and his melds total 210, he is said to need 140. As there are 250 points at stake in the trick-taking, his opponents need 111 to defeat him.

Concession The bidder (possibly disappointed with the widow) may concede defeat without even leading to the first trick, whereupon he pays to each opponent chips to the value of his bid. This is called a 'single *bête*' (see Scoring, below). At the same time, either opponent can propose that the opponents concede, and if the other opponent agrees, the contract is considered made. This might happen if the bidder's melds bring him so close to his contract that it is obvious he must make it. Both opponents must agree, however, before they can concede.

Play

The bidder leads to the first trick, and may lead any card he likes; see p148 for an explanation of tricks and trick-taking. The rules of play are not the usual trick-taking rules, however. A player must follow suit if able. If he is unable to follow suit, and holds a trump, he must play a trump. If another player has already played a trump to the trick, he must still play a trump, but he need not try to win the trick. On the other hand, if a trump led, each player must, if able, play a higher trump than any previously played. This is called 'playing over'.

A trick is won by the highest trump it contains. If it does not contain a trump it is won by the highest card of the suit led. If two cards identical in suit and rank are the highest cards in a trick, the first played wins the trick. The winner of a trick leads to the next.

The bidder collects all the tricks he wins and adds them face down to the cards he buried – they will all count for him in the final settlement. The opponents' tricks are collected into a single pile, and at the end of the deal the two sides agree on the number of points the bidder has made, in melds and tricks.

If he has made as many points as he bid, he has made his contract. If he has scored fewer points he has lost. This is called a 'double *bête*' (see Scoring, below).

Scoring

The scoring values of cards taken in tricks are:

each Ace	eleven points
each 10	ten points
each King	four points
each Queen	three points
each Jack	two points
each 9	no value

Only the 9s have no value when taken in tricks. The winner of the last trick scores a bonus of ten points. The number of points available in trick-taking is therefore 250 points per deal.

The melds and their values are as follows:

Sequences	
Flush (A, 10, K, Q, J of trumps)	150
Royal marriage (K, Q of trumps)	40
Common marriage (K, Q of any other suit)	20

Groups	
Hundred Aces (one Ace of each suit)	100
Eighty Kings (one King of each suit)	80
Sixty Queens (one Queen of each suit)	60
Forty Jacks (one Jack of each suit)	40

Special	
Pinochle (♠Q, ♦J)	40
Dix (9 of trumps, pronounced 'deece')	10

A card used in one meld may not be used as part of another meld in the same category, but may be used as part of a meld in another category. For example, a King or Queen used in a flush, cannot be scored also as a royal marriage, since both melds are in the category of sequences, but both could be used in melds of eighty Kings or sixty Queens, since these melds are in the category of groups. If spades were trumps, ♠Q could be used in all three categories.

Settlement Each player settles with each other at the end of each deal. Players use various scales of payment, some quite unrelated to others. A popular method values the making of a contract from one chip from each opponent for a contract of 300–340, to 19 chips for a contract of over 600. The full scale is:

Contract	Chip value
300–340	1
350–390	3
400–440	7
450–490	10
500–540	13
550–590	16
600+	19

Most players agree that the chip value of the contract is doubled if the trump suit is spades.

The bidder receives from or pays to each opponent according to whether he makes his contract. If the bidder is double bête he pays double.

Strategy The strategy begins with what to bid. It is best to employ a cautious outlook in bidding. Playing and failing to make a contract costs twice as much (because of double bête) than is gained in making it, therefore one needs at least a 2–1 on chance of making a contract before it is worth bidding it. Generally speaking, bidding more than what can almost certainly be made is dangerous.

The first step in evaluating a hand is to count the points to be made from melds. To this must be added the expectation to be made from tricks. It is necessary to hold six or seven trumps, or at least no fewer than five top trumps. There are twelve trumps in all, including two of each rank, including Aces. It is reasonable to expect 10–15 points to be won from each trick won (there being 250 points at stake over 15 tricks, but the two opponents will try to play high-value cards to tricks won by each other). Around 20 points could be added for improvement which might come from the exchange.

The hand illustrated has 280 points in melds (with hearts as trumps): 150 for flush, 100 for hundred Aces, 20 common marriage and 10 for dix. If to this is added about 100 for tricks and 20 for the exchange, a total of 400 points is reached, which would be a possible bid, but 450 would be extravagant.

The discard is the next thing to consider. It is reasonable to seek a two-suited or three-suited hand – a long side suit beside a long trump suit is a good way to ensure making plenty of points for tricks, as opponents use their trumps on your long suit, and you can trump their Aces in a void suit. In the hand above, it is impossible to make a void suit, because that would lose the 100 points for Aces (one cannot discard cards used in melds), but the spade suit is ideal for an attempt to hold a bare Ace in a suit, which is equally good.

Suppose you held the hand above, and picking up the widow found ♣10, ♦10, 9. The discard of the two spade Jacks and ♦9 would improve the hand considerably.

It is possible that the widow will change a player's view of which suit to choose as trumps. For example, suppose the holder of the different hand illustrated below has become bidder with a bid of 350, on the strength of holding 250 in melds, with a flush (hearts as trumps), eighty Kings and a common marriage. The widow holds ♠Q, ♦A, ♣9. By taking ♠Q and ♦A in hand, in exchange for ♣J and ♦9 he will immensely improve his hand. He will now make spades trumps. He gains an extra trump (now six) and another ten points in melds, by virtue of dix, making his meld 260. He needs 90 from tricks to make his contract, and will almost certainly do so, and with spades as trumps will score double for it.

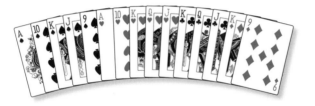

In the play, it is not usually desirable to lead trumps, unless the declarer has a solid side suit, containing, say, both Aces and 10s. In this case leading trumps to exhaust those of the opponents, in order to make the tricks from the side suit at the end, without fear of trumping, might be the policy. With the hand as above, the side suit of hearts is not solid enough, so it would be best to lead the ♦A, then ♥A, followed by, if they win, the ♥J, to try to clear the opponents of hearts and win a long heart or two after winning tricks with the trumps.

Variants

Pinochle for four, five or six players The game can be played by four players by means of one player dropping out in turn and becoming the dealer. The dealer's function is merely to deal the cards for the other players. He does not have cards himself and takes no further part. He is an inactive player, and may not advise either side. The player to his left becomes the eldest hand, and the game proceeds as above. The inactive player does, however, take part in the settlement. The bidder pays to him or collects from him when he wins or loses as he does with the other opponents.

This is a popular version of the game in the USA. In fact, many players regard it as better than when played by three only; perhaps the inactive role of the dealer enables him to attend to his personal needs and maybe to oversee the beer. It is also not unknown for five or six to play this way, with two or three being inactive on each deal. The dealer misses out the player or two to his left when dealing. However many players there are, active and inactive, each player's turn in dealing, bidding and playing comes to him clockwise from his right.

Poker

Poker is often referred to as the national card game of the USA, where its popularity grew from its first mention in reference books in the 1830s to its current ubiquity on the Internet and television screens. The early references to Poker place it as being played around New Orleans, which was French territory until sold to the USA by Napoleon Bonaparte in 1803, leading to the belief that the direct ancestor was the French game Poque. There are now many forms of Poker.

Type	A game of betting and bluffing
Alternative names	None; the main varieties are Draw Poker, Omaha, Stud Poker and Texas Hold 'Em
Players	Any number; five to seven is perhaps best
Special requirements	Chips or cash for staking

Aim

To win money, or chips representing money, by holding the best hand at the end of the deal.

Cards

The standard pack of 52 cards is used, the cards ranking from Ace (high) to 2 (low). The Ace may be used in sequences, called 'straights', as either high or low; for example, A, K, Q, J, 10 and A, 2, 3, 4, 5 are both valid sequences, but Q, K, A, 2, 3 is not.

Preparation

Each player in each deal is dealt a hand of five cards. In some games, for example Seven-card Stud Poker, a player selects his five-card hand from a larger number dealt to him, and in others, such as Texas Hold 'Em, a player will select his hand from cards dealt specifically to him and from others which are communal cards, available to all players. In every case, however, the hand which counts consists of five cards.

Play

In successive rounds of betting, each player has the opportunity to bet that his hand is the best or to 'fold' (ie drop out). Bets are made by players placing their stakes towards the centre of the table, the accumulated stakes forming the 'pot'. At any time during the betting a player may fold, but he loses the stakes he has contributed to the pot. Any player may raise the stakes during the betting, and the other players must equalize the stakes or fold.

The deal is complete when all but one player has folded, in which case he takes the pot, or when all the players remaining have equalized their bets and none wishes to raise the stake higher. In this case there is a 'showdown', when the players reveal their hands and the player with the highest ranking hand wins the pot. If two or more players have equal hands at the showdown, the pot is shared.

Each Poker deal is complete in itself, and settlement is made after each.

Ranks of Poker hands There are nine classes of Poker hand. They are ranked in the following order, along with the number of such possible hands in a 52-card pack, and the probability of being dealt such a hand straight from the pack.

Straight flush (40; 1 in 64,974 or 0.0015%)
Five cards of the same suit in sequence. Between two straight flushes, that with the higher top card wins. A tie is possible. The highest straight flush of all (A, K, Q, J, 10), of which there are only four in the pack, is called a 'royal flush', and in some books this is unnecessarily listed as a class of hand on its own.

Four of a kind (624; 1 in 4,165 or 0.0240%)
Four cards of the same rank, with an odd card. Of similar hands, that with the higher ranking four cards wins. A tie is not possible, so the rank of the odd card is of no consequence.

Full house (3,744; 1 in 694 or 0.1441%)
Three cards of one rank (a 'triple') with two of another (a 'pair'). Between two full houses, that with the higher ranking triple wins. A tie is not possible.

Flush (5,108; 1 in 509 or 0.1967%)
Five cards of the same suit, but not in sequence. Between flushes, that containing the highest card wins, if equal the second highest and so on. A tie is possible.

Straight (10,200; 1 in 255 or 0.3925%)
Five cards in sequence, but not of the same suit. Between straights, that with the highest card at the top of the sequence wins, thus A, K, Q, J, 10 is the highest straight and 5, 4, 3, 2, A the lowest. A tie is possible.

Three of a kind (54,912; 1 in 47 or 2.1129%)
Three cards of the same rank with two unmatching cards. Between similar hands, that with the highest ranking triple wins. A tie is not possible.

Two pairs (123,552; 1 in 21 or 4.7359%)
Two cards of one rank, two of another and an odd card. Between similar hands, that with the higher ranking, top pair wins, if equal that with the higher ranking second pair, if equal the higher ranking odd card. A tie is possible.

One pair (1,098,240; 1 in 2.3665 or 42.2569%)
Two cards of one rank plus three unmatching cards. Between similar hands, that with the highest ranking pair wins, if equal the highest ranking odd card, if equal the highest ranking second odd card, and so on. A tie is possible.

High card (1,302,540; 1 in 1.9953 or 50.1177%)
This hand lacks an accepted name and is sometimes called 'nothing' or 'no pair'. These hands are ranked by the highest ranked card they contain, if equal the second highest ranked, and so on. A tie is possible.

It will be noted that almost exactly half of hands do not contain even one pair, and that over 92% of hands are not better than one pair. However, it should be appreciated that in Draw Poker, with its chance to improve the hand, these percentages are very different after the draw, and in other forms of Poker, where the hand is chosen from, say, seven cards, the percentages also do not apply. The nine classes of hand, with the highest and lowest hands in each class, are shown below and overleaf.

Ranks of Poker hand

Blank cards are immaterial since they cannot affect ties

Example of highest possible   *Example of lowest possible*

Straight flush

Royal flush

Four of a kind

Full house

Flush

Straight

Example of highest possible   *Example of lowest possible*

Three of a kind

Two pairs

One pair

High card

Draw Poker

Draw Poker is the simplest form of Poker played today. It is best for between five and seven players.

Preparation Players should first agree on a time limit. This avoids ill-feeling, when a losing player will not agree to a game ending. After the time limit is passed, any player can announce that the next deal will be his last. Play should end when the deal arrives back at the first dealer.

Agreement should also be reached on minimum and maximum stakes; for example, a minimum of one chip and a maximum of five chips. If they wish, players might also agree on the maximum number of raises any player might make in one betting interval.

To decide the first dealer, and where players are to sit, the cards can be shuffled by one player and cut by another, prior to any player dealing a card face up to all players. The player dealt the highest card is the first dealer and can choose his seat. The next highest chooses his seat, and so on. Players dealt equal cards are dealt a second to break the tie.

Before the deal, each player puts one chip into the centre to form a pot. This is called an 'ante'. If preferred, to streamline matters, the dealer can put in the whole amount of the ante himself.

The dealer shuffles and the player on his right cuts the cards. The dealer then deals five cards to each player one at a time face down clockwise to his left. The dealer places the remainder of the pack face down in front of him.

First betting interval After examining their hands, players have an opportunity to bet, the 'eldest hand' (the player to the dealer's left) first. He has three options: to fold, to 'check' or to bet. To fold, he places his hand face down before him and takes no further part in the deal. To check, he stays in the deal but without staking anything. He announces 'check', but in established games the player usually just taps his fingers on the table. He bets by pushing a stake between the minimum and maximum agreed towards the centre of the table and announcing its amount. At all times players must keep their stakes visible and separate from those of other players so that it is clear how much they have staked.

Each player round the table has the same options until one of them bets. The options then become: to fold, to 'call' or to 'raise'. To call, a player puts in a stake equivalent to the amount of the previous bet. To raise, he puts in the amount needed to call, ie to equal the previous stake, plus a further amount to raise the stake higher. For example, if he needs to put in two chips to call, he can announce 'call for two, and raise two more', placing four chips towards the centre.

Play continues with all players folding, calling or raising until all the players remaining have equal stakes on the table, when the first betting interval ends.

If nobody bets, the deal is abandoned, the cards are collected and the deal passes to the left. The chips in the pot remain for the next deal, and are added to by the players putting in their antes for the next deal.

Draw Placing his own hand face down on the table, the dealer takes up the pack and asks in turn each active player, beginning with the one nearest his left, how many cards he wishes to draw. If he does not wish to draw any he 'stands pat'. Otherwise, he may draw any number from one to three; if there are fewer than six players, he may discard and draw four. He announces how many he wishes, and discards the equivalent number from his hand by passing them face down to the dealer who begins a discard pile to one side of him. He then deals face down to the player the number of cards needed to being his hand back to five cards. All players are dealt with in the same manner, and if the dealer is still active he deals with himself last, showing all other players how many cards he is exchanging.

Before a bet has been made in the second betting interval, any player may ask another how many cards he drew.

Second betting interval When all the players have what is now their final hand, the second betting interval takes place. The first player to speak is the player who opened the betting on the first betting interval, or if he has since folded, the first active player to his left. The procedure is exactly the same as the first betting interval. When all players still active have contributed the same amount to the pot, the betting ends.

Showdown Starting with the last player to raise, and continuing clockwise, the players reveal their hands and the player with the best hand takes the pot. If there is a tie, the pot is shared. If all players fold except one, the winner may take the pot without being obliged to show his hand.

Example hand Hands are dealt to six players as shown.

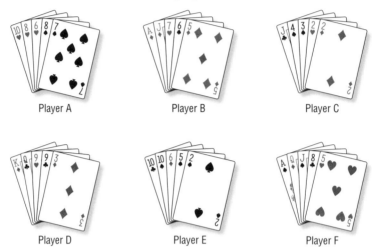

Player A   Player B   Player C

Player D   Player E   Player F

Player A was the dealer, and has put six chips into the pot. The first betting interval proceeds as follows:

1	Player B checks
2	Player C checks
3	Player D bets one chip
4	Player E calls
5	Player F calls
6	Player A calls
7	Player B calls
8	Player C calls

The first betting interval ends with all players active and six chips staked (plus six in the pot). The draw now takes place:

9	Player B keeps ♦ A, J and draws three: ♣A, 2, ♥ J
10	Player C keeps his pair of 2s and draws ♣3, ♥A, 3
11	Player D keeps his pair of 9s and draws ♦ 7, 4, ♣5
12	Player E keeps his pair of 10s and draws ♣K, ♠K, 9
13	Player F keeps ♠A, J, ♦ Q and draws ♦ 10, 8
14	Player A keeps his pair of 8s and draws ♥Q, ♦ 9, ♣4

The new hands are shown below.

Player A	Player B	Player C

Player D	Player E	Player F

In the second betting interval, Player D, as the first to bet on the first betting interval, has the first opportunity to bet:

15	Player D, disappointed at not improving his hand, checks
16	Player E, with two pairs, bets one chip; he is willing to bet more, but does not wish to scare his opponents into folding
17	Player F folds
18	Player A, who also did not improve his pair of 8s, decides to call
19	Player B, with two big pairs, calls one and raises one
20	Player C, who also has two pairs, calls, pushing forward two chips
21	Player D now thinks he is beaten, and folds
22	Player E likes the way things have gone, calls one and raises two
23	Player A now folds
24	Player B calls two and raises a further three
25	Player C, thinking the other two might have only a big pair each, decides to call, thinking this might be his last bet if the others press on; it costs him five chips to call
26	Player E, still thinking he might have the best hand, calls three and raises three more
27	Player B, now fearing Player E has a triple, calls for three
28	Player C has a Poker player's typical dilemma; he fears he has lost but is unwilling to give up when it will cost him only three to call and end the betting. He calls.

As the players have equalized their stakes, Player E shows his hand first, only to find that Player B has beaten him. As he feared, Player C is also beaten and sacrificed his last three chips for nothing. So Player B picks up 43 chips, including the pool of six.

There are many variants of Draw Poker, the most common of which are explained below.

Jackpots Of the many variations on Draw Poker, Jackpots must be mentioned because it is the most popular, and in the USA in particular is often described as if it were the parent game. The difference is that before any player can make a bet, he must hold a pair of Jacks or better. Once a player has opened the betting, other players may call, bet or raise as they wish.

A player who opens the betting must retain his discards and, if he folds, his hand, since at the end of the deal he might be required to prove that he had the requisite two Jacks or better to open. If nobody opens, the hand is abandoned and the deal passes to the next player, with the pot remaining in the centre and being added to by another round of antes.

Progressive Jackpots This is played as Jackpots, except that if a hand is abandoned because nobody can open the betting, the requirement to open on the next hand is a pair of Queens or better ('Queenpots'). Further abandonments lead to the minimums becoming a pair of Kings, then Aces. If the succession of abandoned hands continues after 'Acepots', the minimum requirement to open reduces, to a pair of Kings, then Queens, then Jacks, and then back upwards again... and so on, up and down. Meanwhile, the pot continues growing with each abandoned hand.

Wild cards In all forms of Poker, 'wild cards' can be used. A wild card is a card which can represent any card its holder wishes. At one time, a Joker was added to the pack as a wild card. In modern times it is more usual for a whole rank to be wild, and this is usually the 2s ('deuces wild'). If only two wild cards are required, they can be the black 2s, or some prefer the 'one-eyed Jacks' (♥J and ♠J).

Wild cards are introduced to allow players to hold higher-ranking hands, but they are not recommended, and decisions must be made as to how they are used. For example, can a hand of five of a kind be allowed? Or a flush headed by two Aces, which might be claimed by a player holding ♦A, 9, 7, 4 plus a wild card? These dilemmas can be solved by a rule which prevents a wild card duplicating a card which is already held. This would rule out five of a kind and a doubled-Aced flush.

There is also the question of whether a hand without a wild card beats a hand in the same category which uses one. For example, the straight J, 10, 9, W, 7, where W represents a wild card, would beat the straight 8, 7, 6, 5, 4 unless there were a rule to the contrary. Players must agree these side issues if they wish to play with wild cards.

Spit in the Ocean The distinguishing feature of this form of Poker is that players are dealt four cards each face down, and their hands are completed by a final card which is dealt face up to the centre of the table. This is a card common to all players. However, this card (called the 'spit') is a wild card, as are all three other cards of the same rank. So all players have at least one wild card in their hands, and some may have two, three or four.

The game is usually played with only one betting interval, ie without a draw. However, it can be played as Draw Poker, with betting intervals before and after a draw. Players must decide beforehand the rules governing wild cards.

Lowball Lowball is played as Draw Poker, but with the great difference that it is the lowest-ranked hand which wins. The ranking of the hands is different. Flushes and straights are ignored, and Ace counts low in all respects.

Thus the lowest hand (and therefore a winning hand) is 5, 4, 3, 2, A, the lowest ranked cards in the pack. It does not count as a straight, and if all the cards were the same suit, it would not count as a flush.

Where unmatched hands are concerned (ie those not containing a pair, a triple or a four, the highest-ranking card determines the precedence and, if equal, the next highest and so on (exactly as it does in Draw Poker). For example, 9, 6, 5, 4, 3 beats 9, 8, 4, 3, 2 in Lowball, because the 6 is lower than the 8.

All the procedures, for example the two betting intervals, one each side of the draw, are the same as in Draw Poker.

High-Low Poker This form of Poker is a combination of the standard game in which the highest-ranked hand wins, and Lowball, in which the lowest wins. The pot is shared by the highest hand and the lowest (an odd chip going to the highest) and players can go for either, or even for both, as the same hand can win both (as will be explained).

Players do not declare until the showdown whether they are trying to win high or low. A player drawing two cards to 3, 2, A, hoping for low, might draw two Aces, and immediately be hoping to win high.

High hands are ranked as in Draw Poker, and low as in Lowball, which accounts for the possibility of one hand winning both, for example ♥A, 7, 6, 4, 2 would have an excellent chance of winning high as an Ace flush, and of winning low as 7 high.

At the showdown, before exposing their hands, players must indicate simultaneously whether they are trying for high or low. The simplest way of doing this is for each player to hide a chip in his fist under the table, say blue for high, white for low, one of each for high-low (ie high and low). Players then unclench their fists at the same time to indicate which pot they are aiming at.

If only one player is trying for high or low, he wins his half of the pot automatically. If all the players try for the same pot (for example if there are three in the showdown and all go for high) then the winner takes the whole pot. This, obviously, leads to some interesting choices for players. A player aiming for high, for example, but judging from the betting that he is unlikely to win, might at the showdown opt instead to go for low, hoping that he will be the only one who does.

A player who competes for high-low must have the best hand in both categories to win. If he holds the highest hand but not the lowest, or vice-versa, he loses both. The other players take the pots as if he hadn't bet.

Dealer's Choice Poker is a rapidly evolving game in which dozens of variants have been recorded (and no doubt thousands unrecorded). One of the popular versions in social games, where the players know each other and all the variants, is to have a session of Dealer's Choice. In this, each dealer chooses which variant will be played on his deal. It introduces variety and keeps everybody on their toes.

Stud Poker

The main difference between Stud Poker and Draw Poker is that in Stud Poker most of the cards are dealt face up and there is no draw. There are two forms, five-card and seven-card.

Five-card Stud Poker It is possible for up to ten people to play Stud Poker, but it is better for up to six. Even as few as two can play, as the marathon match which was at the centre of the film *The Cincinnati Kid* showed.

As with Draw Poker, the seating, first dealer, time limit and stake limits for Stud Poker should be agreed beforehand. It is not usual to have an ante, but some players like to have one. A way of limiting stakes is to make the lowest bet of one chip, with high limits varying with the betting intervals, say two for the first, three for the second, four for the third and six for the fourth and last. It is usual for the high limit to come into force on any round after a player has an 'open pair', ie a pair among his cards face up on the table.

After the shuffle and cut, the dealer deals one card face down to each player (his 'hole card'). He then deals one card face up to each, and the first betting interval takes place. The player with the highest face-up card is the first to bet. If there are equal highest cards showing, the holder of the one nearest the dealer's left bets first. This player has no option. He is obliged to bet within the staking limits agreed. Thereafter, each player in turn may fold, call or raise. Betting continues until all the stakes of those still active are equalized. A player who folds must turn his face-up card (or later, cards) face down and place it on his hole card. At no time may other players see these cards.

The dealer then deals a second face up card to each active player. There is then a second betting interval. Again the player whose face-up cards show the highest Poker combination has first opportunity to bet. For this purpose, straights and flushes do not count, so in the second betting interval a pair is the highest combination possible (on later rounds, it might be a triple or four, but flushes and straights never count). From the second betting interval onwards, the first player, and subsequently others, may 'check', ie stay in without betting, but once a player has bet, that option disappears and players must fold, call or raise.

When stakes are equalized again, a third card is dealt face down, followed by a betting interval, and then a fourth, followed by the last betting interval.

When dealing the face-up cards, the dealer should announce the rank of the receiving player's hand, for example he should say 'Queen high' or 'pair of 9s', etc, and at the end of that round of dealing point out which player must speak first in the betting interval. If he makes a mistake, other players may correct him. On the third and fourth rounds, he should also announce possible flushes or straights, for example dealing a 10 to a hand consisting of a Jack and 9, he should say 'possible straight'. He is not liable for any errors he makes and players can correct him if he makes one.

If, before the final cards are dealt, all players have folded except one, then that player takes the pot without the need to show his hole card. If after the fourth betting interval there are two or more players remaining, there is a showdown in which each player turns over his hole card, the hands are compared, and the player with the best takes the pot.

Seven-card Stud Poker Seven-card Stud Poker (also known as Seven-toed Pete or Down the River) is very popular, and perhaps the most interesting form of Poker for home play. Seven players is the maximum.

The preparations are as for Five-card Stud, except that the betting limits are not affected by the appearance of a pair among a player's cards.

After the shuffle, the dealer deals one card face down to each player, then another, and then one card face up. Each player has two hole cards. As with Five-card Stud, the player with the highest face-up card is obliged to bet, and subsequent players to fold, call or raise. After the bets are equalized, a second face-up card is dealt to all players, and a second betting interval takes place, with this time the player with the highest combination showing having the right to check, as in Five-card Stud. Play proceeds as in Five-card Stud, with face-up cards being dealt one at a time, followed by a betting interval, until each player has two hole cards and four face-up cards. After this betting interval, a seventh card is dealt to each player face down, giving each player three hole cards. There follows the final betting interval and the showdown, if necessary, during which each player reveals his hole cards and makes the best Poker hand he can from the seven available to him. The player with the best hand takes the pot.

Variants on Stud Poker There are many variants on Stud Poker. The game can be played Lowball, and High-low, with the rankings for the low hands being as described in Lowball and High-Low Draw Poker, with the players making their calls of high or low or both in the same manner, with chips of different colours.

Seven-card Stud, High-Low This is a very interesting game, guaranteeing plenty of action, and an example hand is given below. Five hands are dealt as shown:

			Face-up cards				
Player	Hole cards		1	2	3	4	Final hole card
A	♣8 ♦7		♠6	♦6	♦J	♣5	♦A
B	♠K ♦8		♣K	♦3	♦10	♥3	♦K
C	♠5 ♥5		♠9	♦4	♣Q	♥A	
D	♥K ♠10		♥10	♣6	♥2	♦5	
E	♠Q ♥7		♠J	♦Q	♠A	♣3	♣7

The limits are one chip minimum, three chips maximum for the first three betting intervals and five for the last two.

After the first face-up card is dealt, Player B with a King showing is the first to bet, and he must bet, so he bets one chip. All players call. Three players have pairs already, Player C's being concealed. Player A has every chance of a straight, and with 8 high is best placed at the moment for low.

The second face-up card leaves Player A with a pair showing, so he speaks first. He is allowed to check, but decides to bet one chip, as he likes the look of his hand. Again, all the players call. Three of them have pairs higher than Player A's 6s, and Player C, who was dealt a pair, is actually last on the current ranking of the hands. Of course, each player can see only the face-up cards of their opponents, and no hand looks impressive yet, judging by the cards on the table. Even Player A's exposed pair of 6s does not look very good, as a third 6 is already exposed on the table in Player D's hand.

The third face-up card leaves Player A, showing two 6s, the first to bet again. Nobody has improved on this round, so betting is cautious. Players B and D have three cards towards a flush. Player A checks. Player B raises one chip and all others call.

The fourth face-up card leaves Player A still the first to speak. His straight is still a possibility and if his last hole card is 3, 2, or Ace he will have 8 high for low. He decides to check.

Player B now has two pairs, and there isn't another King on the table. He decides to bet five. It is something of a bluff. He doubts if another holds a triple, and hopes to scare off all high contenders. Player C decides low is his only chance, and he cannot do better than 9 high, so he folds. Player D also folds, thinking his pair of 10s will not win high and not fancying his chance of low. Player E decides to call. He could go high if he gets an Ace or a Queen, or try low with Jack high if he gets a low card. Player A, with only two others remaining in, and possibilities of high or low, also calls.

The final hole cards were excellent for Player A and Player B. Player A, certain he thinks of low, bets five. Player B cannot see himself beaten for high with a full house, calls and raises five. Player E, despite getting ♣7 and thus two pairs, guesses that Player B has cards on the table to beat his hand for high and is not going to bet ten more chips on low as Player A is almost certainly going to call low, so he folds. Player A calls.

Player A calls low and Player B high. They do not have to show their hands to share the pot, each taking 25 chips, and each therefore winning seven chips on the deal. It might not seem much, having put 18 each in themselves, but once they began staking in five chips at a time, they were pretty sure of winning.

English Seven-card Stud This interesting version of Stud introduces a drawing element. It is played as Seven-card Stud described above until the stage when all players have five cards, two 'in the hole' and three face up. At this stage, players reject one card before receiving their sixth card from the dealer. They may reject a hole card or a face-up card. If they reject a hole card, the sixth card is dealt to them face down, but if they reject a face-up card, the sixth card is dealt face up. After the betting interval, the seventh card is dealt to them in the same way. Therefore a player's hand is never more than five cards, two face down and three face up. On the sixth and seventh rounds, a player happy with his hand need not draw a new card at all – he can stand pat with the five cards he has. If he stands pat on the sixth round, he must do so on the seventh round as well.

Texas Hold 'Em

This is the form of Poker which has had the greatest explosion in popularity since the 1980s, when World Championships began to be played in US casinos, in particular Binion's Horseshoe in Las Vegas. Once television channels on both sides of the Atlantic began hosting big-money tournaments, and then celebrity tournaments, the public took to the game in a big way and now thousands play on the Internet.

Texas Hold 'Em, often just called Hold 'Em, can be played in theory by up to 22 players (ie there are enough cards in the pack to accommodate 22 players), but in practice six to eight is best. In this form of Poker, each player's object is to make the best possible Poker hand from the two cards he holds and the five common cards, called 'community cards', which are dealt in stages to the table. A player may use both his cards, or one, or none, as he prefers. Of course, if he uses none (called 'playing the board') he cannot do better than tie, since all the other players have the same option to use all five community cards as their hands.

Preparation The first dealer and the seating arrangement are decided in the manner described for Draw Poker.

Stake Limits Before each deal the first two players to the left of the dealer put towards the centre small stakes known as 'blind bets' or 'blinds'. The first player puts in a 'small blind', which would be one chip. The next player puts in a 'big blind', which might be any multiple of the small blind, and is usually three chips. This will make the minimum stake for betting and raising three chips. The maximum bet and raise can be what players decide. It is best to have a maximum, say ten or twenty chips, or the richest player will be able to steamroller his opponents with huge bets.

In televised tournaments there is no limit, but all players start with the same amount of chips and retire when they lose them. These are knockout tournaments, and allowing each player the same amount of chips to start makes it a fair tournament. In tournaments of this kind, the blind bets get progressively bigger. This speeds up the betting, in effect forcing players to bet more than they would otherwise, and ensuring a result in a reasonable amount of time. Social players can play like this, but generally prefer a game where some win and some lose, rather than a winner-takes-all game.

When the two players to the dealer's left have made the blind bets, the dealer shuffles and the player to his right cuts. The dealer deals clockwise one card at a time face down to each player, including himself, until all players have two cards.

In casinos, and televised tournaments, a dealer, who does not take part in the game, is provided, so that the players do not have to deal themselves. In effect, the dealer deals for each player in turn. A disc, or 'button', is moved round the table on each deal to indicate which player is the 'dealer', and thus which players must put in the blinds.

Play The first player to speak is the player to the left of big blind. He cannot check, because the blind bets are regarded as normal bets, so he must fold, call or raise. All players in turn have the same options, including the blind bettors. Small blind must obviously add to his stake if he wishes to stay in, since he contributed only one chip to the pot. Big blind will have to increase his stake to stay in too, if the stake has been raised before his turn comes round.

When all the stakes are equalized, the dealer deals three cards face up to the table in a row. These are known as the 'flop', and are common to all players, who now have five cards each. There is now a second betting interval, in which the first to speak is the nearest active player to the dealer's left, as is the case on subsequent betting intervals. A player may check on this round, as all the stakes are equal, but as soon as a player bets, then all others must either fold, call or raise.

When stakes are equalized, a fourth card is dealt to the row on the table. This is called the 'turn', or 'fourth street'. A third betting interval takes place, after which a final card is dealt to the row of community cards. This is 'fifth street' or 'the river'.

The final betting interval takes place, and if necessary there is a showdown.

93

Tournament play In the tournaments, as widely televised, the only limit is the amount of chips a player has, and often a player's best policy is to go 'all in', ie to bet all his chips at once. Any active players can now only fold or call, and if anyone calls there is a showdown, which will result in the player who went all in being eliminated if his hand is not the best.

Example hand Six players are dealt two hole cards each, as in the illustration that follows.

Small blind is one chip, big blind three and the maximum bet and raise is twelve chips. Player A is the dealer, so Player B stakes one chip as small blind and Player C three chips as big blind.

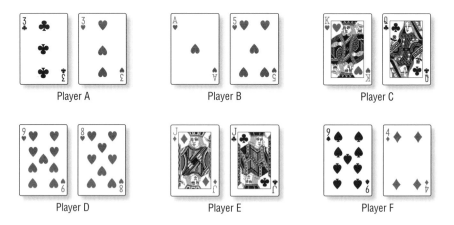

| Player A | Player B | Player C |
| Player D | Player E | Player F |

Player D speaks first, and with 9, 8 'suited' (ie of the same suit) he calls with three chips. Player E has a good hand, a medium pair (Jacks) and also calls. Player F folds. Player A calls with his small pair. He will be hoping for a third 3 on the flop, as a small pair is not likely to win anything unless it improves. Player B has a suited Ace, a reasonable hand, and calls. As he has already staked one chip, it costs him two chips to call. Stakes are equalized, and the dealer deals the flop. This is shown below.

Flop

Player B speaks first on the next betting interval. He has not improved, but has three hearts towards a flush. He checks. Player C has a pair of Queens and a Jack on fourth or fifth street would give him a straight. He bets three chips. Player D has a pair of 9s, not too impressive in itself, but he also requires a Jack for a straight, and calls. Player E, who has two Jacks already, also has four cards to a straight, but his is open-ended, and he needs a King or an 8 to complete it. He, too, calls. Player A, with four players still in, decides his two 3s are going nowhere and folds. Player B now has to decide whether to risk three more chips on seeing fourth street, and being adventurous, he calls and stays in.

The dealer adds the turn, or fourth street, to the flop. It is ♥10, and the community cards are as shown below. The pair of 10s in the community cards make everybody's hands look better, but in fact, everybody has this pair.

Flop and turn

Player B speaks first. His only realistic chance of winning this hand is if a fourth heart appears on the river. He would then have an outstanding chance of winning, as he would hold the best possible flush, as he has the Ace. The best possible flush, as the cards lie, is known as the 'nut' flush. He would beat any straight that another might hold. But, in reality, he has only a pair of 10s at the moment. He decides to check. Player C has two pairs (although everybody has the 10s) and stakes another three chips on his hand. Player D needs only the ♥J on the street to hold every player's dream, a straight flush. From his point of view, the odds against him getting it on the river are 45 to 1 (he knows where six cards are, so there are 46 that could appear on the river). Otherwise he holds two pairs and a chance of a straight. He, too, calls. Player E has two pairs, Jacks and 10s, but knows this would be beaten by an opponent whose hole cards included a Queen. He still has a chance of a straight and decides to call. Player B now assesses his chances. There are 46 cards he knows nothing of, of which nine could be hearts. The odds against him getting a heart on the street are 37–9, or roughly 4–1. There are 36 chips in the pot to win, and he needs to put in three to stay in with a chance. As he would be paid out at 12–1 for a 4–1 shot, he decides to call (although, of course, even if a heart appears on the street, he could still lose to a full house which, as the cards lay, and the betting has progressed, is far from an impossibility).

So with four players still in, the dealer turns up the last of the community cards, the river. It is ♠4, which helps nobody. The five common cards are shown below.

Flop, turn and river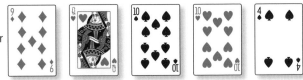

Player B checks but is not going to add to the pot. Player C bets three more, on the strength that if two pairs wins, he probably will, as he can be beaten only by a player with A, A, or K, K, or A, Q as his hole cards. As it happens, Players D and E each have two pairs, and both are reluctant to fold their hands when with three chips they could stay in, so both call. Player B folds. There is a showdown, and Player C discovers he judged his last bet very well, and won an extra six chips from it. He picks up 48 chips, a profit of 36.

Omaha

Omaha is a similar game to Texas Hold 'Em, and in fact the names of these games aren't yet set in stone, and not all books would agree that Omaha is played as described below, or that the game described is Omaha. The main difference to Texas Hold 'Em is that each player has four hole cards instead of two.

95

Preparation The choice of dealer, shuffle and cut are as described in Texas Hold 'Em. The anteing can be the same (ie small blind and big blind), or the method described under Draw Poker can be used, with each player contributing an ante or the dealer putting in a chip for each player.

The dealer deals four cards face down to each player one at a time clockwise. Players examine their cards and a betting interval takes place. The first to speak at this and succeeding betting intervals is always the first active player to the left of the dealer, except when the small and big blind system of antes is used when, at the first betting interval only, the player to the left of big blind speaks first.

When all bets are equalized, the first three community cards, the flop, are dealt in a row. A second betting interval takes place, then the turn is revealed, followed by a third betting interval, which is followed by the exposure of the river and the final betting interval. These procedures are exactly the same as described for Texas Hold 'Em.

There is now a showdown, which is where there is a further difference to Texas Hold 'Em. Each player has nine cards from which to select his best hand, but there is a vital restriction. Each player must use two of his four hole cards to build his hand, together with three of the five community cards. The holder of the best hand at the showdown wins the pot.

Example hand The need to use precisely two hole cards and three community cards causes problems which can spoil promising hands.

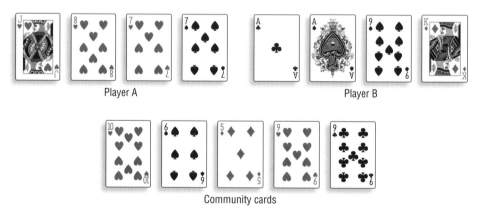

Player A   Player B

Community cards

Suppose two players remain for the showdown, with the hands shown above. Player A, could he use all nine cards available to him, would hold a straight flush, with ♥J, 10, 9, 8, 7. But he can use only two of ♥J, 8, 7 which he holds in his hand. Player B, with unrestricted choice of the nine cards, could have a full house, with ♠9, ♣9, ♥9, ♣A, ♠A. But he cannot use both Aces plus a 9 from his hand.

The best hands the players can make are shown below, with Player A having the better: a straight opposed to a triple.

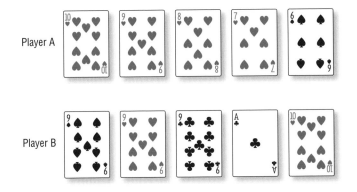

Player A

Player B

Omaha High-Low Eight This variant of Omaha is an interesting game. It is played as other High-low Poker games, with half the pot going to the high hand and half to the low hand. The number of cards to choose from, plus the restriction of having to use two hole cards and three community cards in each hand, make for many permutations of hands and the fact that a player can go for high or low with completely different hands makes it fascinating. The 'Eight' in the title refers to another restriction: that the low hand has to be no worse than 8 high in order to compete, ie a 9-high low hand is ineligible.

In the assessment of low hands, flushes and straights do not count, and Ace is low, so that 5, 4, 3, 2, A is the lowest possible hand. A player does not need to specify at the showdown whether he is aiming at high or low, and all players remaining at the showdown provide a hand for each. If no players in the showdown can compete for low because they do not have a hand which qualifies, then the winner of high takes the whole pot. In the hands shown previously in the example game at Omaha, neither player would have been able to compete for low because there are not three cards among the community cards below the rank of 8.

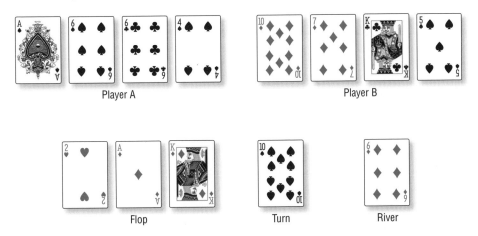

Player A   Player B

Flop   Turn   River

The illustration shows the four hole cards of two players at the showdown, together with the community cards. Player A, because of the restriction of having to use two hole cards only, cannot make a full house for high despite having three 6s and two

Aces in his total of nine cards. His best hand is a triple of 6s. Player B wins high on the strength of his flush in diamonds.

Player A is even more unlucky when it comes to low. Despite his nine cards including no fewer than seven with a rank of 6 or under, he cannot make a hand eligible for low, as he has only four cards of different ranks below 8 in 6, 4, 2, A. He cannot use another Ace or 6 because that would give him a pair. Player B, on the other hand, can win low with ♦7, ♦6, ♠5, ♥2, ♦A. Not that he needed to; he would take the whole pot anyway by virtue of winning high, and Player A failing to win low.

General strategy in Poker

Psychology and bluff probably play bigger roles in Poker than in any other card game, but it would be wrong to believe, as many non-players might believe, that bluffing and a 'poker face' are the main elements of the game. It is possible to win at Poker without bluffing, but it is impossible to win without a grasp of the arithmetic possibilities of the game: the value of a hand, the probabilities of improving it, what might be inferred from the number of cards opponents draw and how they bet. A knowledge of the ranks of the combinations of two cards that might be held as the hole cards – for example that a pair of Aces is much better than a pair of Kings, which is considerably better than a pair of Queens, and that Jacks, 10s and 9s should be considered only as medium pairs, and that an Ace with a high kicker, particularly if suited, is more valuable than a small pair – is worth more to a player than any supposed skill at bluffing.

So far as bluffing is concerned, there are two main objectives. One is to mislead your opponents into believing that your hand is better than it is. The object is to persuade them to fold, so that you win without a showdown. This is more likely to succeed if there is only one opponent to beat, therefore is best practised by a player speaking last when all but one have folded. To bluff with a poor hand when speaking first, and then finding two or three opponents calling or raising, is a good way to lose money pointlessly.

The other objective in bluffing is more subtle, and probably more used and more successful. It is used to fool opponents into believing that your hand is not so good. Should a player on receiving a good hand bet the maximum, or make the maximum raise, players with a middling hand will fold. On the other hand, should he merely call and generally give the impression that he is staying in to see what develops, other players will be encouraged to stay in too, and the pot will grow to a size more worth winning.

There are points to remember about bluffing. One is that one should not become stereotyped. Players who play regularly together will get to know something of each other's habits; it will be noticed if a player always tends to bluff in certain situations, and the bluff will become increasingly less effective. Another is to be decisive. In trying to persuade an opponent your hand is better than it is, there is no point in making a small raise, thinking you'll cut your losses if he calls – a sort of 'each-way' bet. A bluff should be sufficiently high to say to the opponent: 'It will cost all that to see what I've got – are you prepared to risk it?'

The best advice with regard to bluffing is that all bluffs should have a definite purpose, which is winning the pot, and as large a pot as possible. It is a recipe for disappointment to bluff in hope, or in desperation during a run of bad hands.

Pontoon

Pontoon is probably a corruption of the French *Vingt-Un*, through the intermediate stage of Van John, which it was also called. It is likely that British soldiers of World War I picked up the name of the French version. This popular family gambling game often appears in British card books as Vingt-et-Un, although 99% of Britons actually know it as Pontoon. Blackjack is the much less interesting commercial version played in casinos, particularly in the USA. As with many games popular in pubs and houses, rules differ everywhere. Described here is a standard version.

Type	A private banking game
Alternative names	Blackjack, Twenty-One, Vingt-et-Un, Vingt-Un
Players	Three to ten; five or six is best
Special requirements	Chips or coins for staking

Aim
To build a hand to beat the banker, which, apart from special hands, is a hand with a count nearer to, but not exceeding, 21.

Cards
The standard pack of 52 cards is used. Cards have their pip values, with court cards counting as ten, and Aces as one or eleven at their holder's discretion.

Preparation
Any player may pick up the cards, shuffle and begin to deal cards one at a time to each player round the table until a Jack appears. The player dealt the Jack becomes the first dealer, who is also the banker.

There is an advantage to holding the bank. The bank passes from one player to another on the occurrence of a special hand called a 'pontoon', as will be explained below.

It is as well to agree a minimum and maximum initial stake which can be bet on a card.

Play
The banker deals one card face down to each player, including himself. The players look at their cards but the banker does not. Each player announces a stake and places it before him. It should be between an agreed minimum and maximum. The banker then gives each player, and himself, a second face-down card. Again, the players look at their cards but the banker does not.

Players try to build a hand with a pip value of 21, or as near to it as possible without exceeding it. If a player holds a 'pontoon' (a two-card hand of 21, consisting of an Ace and a 10-count card) he declares it immediately and lays it on the table, usually with one card exposed. This is the highest hand and cannot be beaten, except by the banker also holding a pontoon.

The banker then deals with each player in turn, beginning with the player to his left.

A player who has been dealt a pair of Aces may 'split' them. He separates the cards and puts the same stake on the second card as on the first. The two cards now represent the first cards of two hands, so the banker deals a second card to each hand and deals with them separately. A player splitting Aces who receives another Ace to either hand can split further, and could (very rarely) hold four separate hands.

Each player has three choices when the banker comes to deal with him. He may:

Stand or stick	This means he is happy with his count and stands or sticks with it, taking no more cards. He may not stand on a total lower then 16.
Buy	He may buy a further card face down, for a stake not exceeding his previous stake. He can buy further cards if he wishes, but always for a stake not exceeding his previous one. He may continue to buy until he has five cards, which is a special hand. A five-card hand, no matter what its total, beats all other hands except a pontoon. A player cannot buy a fifth card if his four-card total is 11 or lower. This is because he cannot lose, as he cannot exceed 21. He may, however, 'twist', which is to receive another card without buying it.
Twist	This is a request that the dealer twist the player a card face up, for which he does not pay. A player may twist at any time, whether or not he has previously bought a card, but he cannot buy a card after he has twisted.

If while receiving cards a player's count exceeds 21, he has 'busted' and loses his stake. He passes his hand to the banker, who puts it face down on the bottom of the pack. He also passes over his stake.

When all the players have been dealt with (they do not show their hands), the banker turns over his two cards. If he has a pontoon, he immediately takes all the stakes of the players remaining in the game, including any players who also have a pontoon. Otherwise he may stand, or deal himself extra cards, standing when he wishes to. There is no restriction on when he may stand.

If the banker has a five-card hand, he loses to a pontoon but beats all other hands, including a player's five-card hand. Thus, should his count be 21, he will announce he is paying pontoons and five-card tricks only.

The banker wins on all ties.

Should the banker's count exceed 21, he busts and pays all players still in the game.

A player who holds a pontoon is paid double by the banker, except when the pontoon was part of a split hand. The banker is not paid double when he holds a pontoon, nor is a banker allowed to split Aces (he may still count them as 1 or 11).

The banker holds the bank until a player beats him with a pontoon, when that player may take over the bank if he wishes (he should, as it is usually profitable). Should two or more players hold a pontoon on the same deal, the player nearest to the banker's left has precedence.

The reason the bank is usually profitable, despite the fact that the players can choose their stakes according to their hands, is that the banker wins all tied hands, and wins from all players who bust, even though he might bust himself.

See Example hand, overleaf.

Variants

i)   A common variant is to allow a third category of hand, a 'prial' of 7s, ie three 7s. This hand beats all. When held by a player the banker pays treble, but not vice-versa. Some regard this as unnecessary and feel it detracts from the best hand, pontoon, which after all is the name of the game.

ii) The banker looks at his first card when all players have staked on theirs, and may if he wishes demand all players double their stakes. This just gives him an additional advantage and is not recommended.

iii) An Ace and 10 is not regarded as a pontoon, which is limited to Ace and court card. Ace and 10 count as a normal 21.

iv) The banker is paid double when he holds a pontoon, except by a player holding a pontoon, who just loses his stake. This is not recommended for the same reason as ii) above.

v)   Any pair may be split like Aces. This generally favours the Banker, as it is not a good policy for the player to split cards other than Aces.

vi) The banker looks at his two-card hand before dealing with the players, and if he holds a pontoon exposes it and collects all stakes immediately. This is greatly in favour of the players, who avoid buying cards or splitting Aces in situations when they cannot win.

Pontoon

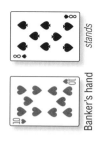

Banker's hand — *stands*

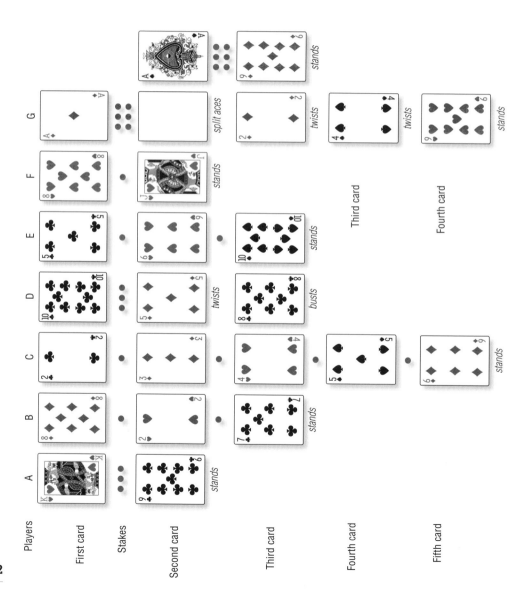

Players	A	B	C	D	E	F	G	
First card	K♥	8♦	2♣	10♣	5♣	8♥	A♦	A♠
Stakes								
Second card	9♣ *stands*	2♥	3♦	5♦ *twists*	6♥	J♣ *stands*	*split aces*	9♦ *stands*
Third card		7♣ *stands*	4♥	8♣ *busts*	10♠ *stands*		2♦ *twists*	
Fourth card			5♥				4♠ *twists*	
Fifth card			9♦ *stands*				6♥ *stands*	

Example hand

The illustration opposite shows how a deal with seven players might progress.

Player A stood on a two-card hand of 19.

Player B bought another card with a two-card total of 10, hoping for a 10-count card, but had to stand with 17.

Player C kept buying cards and was rewarded with a five-card hand.

Player D twisted (he is not allowed to stand) with the nasty count of 15, and bust.

Player E bought a second card with a count of 11 and was rewarded with a 10-count card for a total of 21.

Player F stood on a two-card hand of 18.

Player G split his Aces and eventually stood on both hands with disappointing counts of 16 and 20. He might have stood on the first, by counting his Ace as 11, with a total of 17, but twisted another card in the cope of a five-carder, only to get a 9 and settle with a count of 16, not risking busting in an attempt to get a five-carder.

The banker paid out on hands of 19 and over. So Player A won three units, Player B lost two, Player C won four, Player D lost three, Player E won two, Player F lost one, and Player G lost six on one hand, and won six on the other. The banker lost three units on the deal.

Pope Joan

There is a reference to the game Pope Joan as far back as 1732, and it is the forerunner of Newmarket. Pope Joan was once believed to have been a female pope of the ninth century, and she is represented in the game by the ♦9. The game was very popular in Scotland, and the fact that Scottish feeling against Catholicism was so strong is one of the most widely held beliefs for the fact that the ♦9 is still known as the 'curse of Scotland'.

Type	A game of the Stops family
Alternative names	None
Players	Three to eight
Special requirements	Chips or cash for staking; a board or eight labelled saucers to hold the stakes

Aim
To win the chips in each of the eight divisions on the board by playing the relevant cards or by playing all your cards to the table.

Cards
The standard pack of 52 cards is used, from which is removed the ♦8. Cards rank from King (high) to Ace (low).

Preparation
Pope Joan was traditionally played with an elaborate and highly decorated wooden board, a few of which are still around in museums or maybe antique shops. The circular board contained eight hollows into which chips or counters could be placed as stakes. Nowadays, unless one is lucky enough to own such a board, one must either draw on a sheet of cardboard eight spaces labelled Ace, King, Queen, Jack, Pope (or ♦9), Matrimony, Intrigue and Game, or perhaps place eight saucers on the table carrying those labels. These are spaces into which chips or cash are placed.

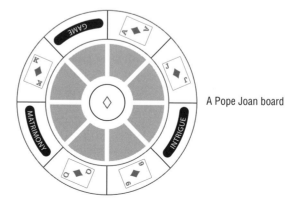

A Pope Joan board

If chips are used, the cash value of each chip should be agreed. Before the deal, the dealer places chips onto the board (or into the saucers) as follows: six in that labelled Pope, two each in Matrimony and Intrigue, and one each in Ace, King, Queen, Jack and Game. This is called 'dressing the board'. It follows that, to be fair, the game should continue until all players have dealt an equal number of times.

Any player may pick up the cards, shuffle and begin to deal cards one at a time to each player round the table until a Jack appears. The player dealt the Jack becomes the first dealer. The deal subsequently passes to the left.

The dealer deals the cards one at a time clockwise to each player. The number of cards each player receives depends on the number of players. Some cards must be left over for a 'widow'. The number of cards to each player and to the widow (spare cards not used) are as follows:

Number of players	Cards each	Widow
3	15	6
4	11	7
5	9	6
6	8	3
7	7	2
8	6	3

The widow is placed face down in the centre and the top card is turned over to denote the 'trump' suit. This is not a trump in the normal sense of the word. It indicates that whoever plays the Ace, King, Queen or Jack of that suit during the game wins the stakes in the appropriate space on the board, or from the appropriate saucer. If the turn-up is itself an Ace, King, Queen or Jack, the dealer immediately wins the stakes on that space.

If the turn-up is the ♦9, the dealer collects the chips in the space labelled Pope or ♦9, and the chip for game. In this case, the hands are not played out. The cards are collected and re-shuffled with the next dealer dressing the board in full before dealing.

Play

The 'eldest hand' (the player to the dealer's left) makes a lead by placing a card in front of him and announcing it. It can be of any suit he chooses, but it must be the lowest card he holds in that suit. The player holding the next card in that suit in ascending sequence then plays it and announces it, then the player with the next card, and so on. For example, if the lead is ♥2, the player with ♥3 plays it, then the player with ♥4 and so on. Sooner or later the sequence will stop, either because it reaches the King, or because the card required is in the widow. The ♦7 is always a stopper, because the ♦8 has been removed from the pack. A player can lay two or more cards on one turn, for example if he holds ♥2, 3, 4 he can play them all at once. A player holding a card eligible for play must play it – in other words, it is illegal to hold up a card which might lead to another player collecting the chips in any category.

When a run is brought to a stop, the player who played the last card begins a new sequence. It can be in the same suit or another, but the card led must be the lowest he holds in the suit.

If a player lays the Ace, King, Queen or Jack of the trump suit, he collects the chips from the appropriate place. If he lays the Pope (♦9) he collects those chips. If he plays both Queen and King of the trump suit he collects as a bonus the chips from the Matrimony space, and if he plays the Jack and Queen of the trump suit he collects the chips from the Intrigue space.

Finally, the first player to get rid of all his cards collects the chip from the Game space, and the game ends. He also collects one chip from each of the other players for each card they still hold in their hands, although an unlucky player caught with the ♦9 in his hand – and who has therefore missed his opportunity to win the large number of chips for Pope – is excused the additional annoyance of having to cough up any chips for his failure to go out.

Any chips not collected from the board at the end of the hand remain there for the next one, in addition to the new chips added by the next dealer when he dresses the board.

Variants

Some players prefer not to bother ensuring that all players start with the same number of cards. Instead they deal an extra hand (the hand after the dealer's) which becomes the widow. It means there are more cards in the widow and fewer in the hands when compared to the table above. With eight players, for example, some players will get only five cards.

Some players prefer that rather than the dealer dress the board, each player distributes chips on the board before each deal. For example, one method is for each player to put three chips in Pope, two each in matrimony and intrigue and one each in the other categories. Another method is for players to stake one chip in all categories.

Some players require a player beginning a new sequence to change the suit colour from the previous sequence. Others allow a player to begin a new sequence with whatever card he likes, not restricting him to the lowest he holds in a suit, but this can be seen to destroy the whole point of the game.

Preference

Preference is a gambling game popular in Central and Eastern Europe and Russia. It is a trick-taking game which includes an auction in which the suits are ranked in an unusual manner. The game described here is a Westernized version published in Germany in 1975.

Type	A trick-taking game
Alternative names	None
Players	Three
Special requirements	Chips or cash for staking, a bowl or saucer for holding the pool of stakes

Aim

To win chips by making enough tricks as declarer to land your contract, or, if a defender, to defeat the declarer.

Cards

The standard pack of 52 cards is used, from which are removed the 6s, 5s, 4s, 3s and 2s, leaving a pack of 32 cards. The cards rank from Ace (high) to 7 (low). The suits are also ranked with hearts (known as the suit of 'preference') the highest, followed by diamonds, clubs and spades in that order.

Preparation

The value of the basic staking unit (ie one chip if chips are used) should be agreed.

Players each draw a card from a spread pack to determine the first dealer. Cards rank for this purpose from ♥A to ♠7, so there cannot be a tie.

It is customary to establish a pot from which winning declarers take their winnings and to which losing declarers add their losses. The winnings and losses will be the value of the trump suit (hearts 4, diamonds 3, clubs 2, hearts 1) multiplied by a figure which must be agreed. Five is a reasonable figure. Since this means a winning declarer in hearts will take out 20 chips, a pot of 45 chips (15 per player) would allow at least two successful hearts declarations before the pot needs to be replenished.

The dealer deals three cards face down to each player clockwise, then one card to a 'talon', followed by four cards to each player and another to the talon, followed by three more to each player. Each player therefore has ten cards and the talon two, all face down.

Bidding A bid is a promise to make the majority of the tricks, ie six or more, with the suit named as trumps. The 'eldest hand' (the player to the dealer's left) begins the bidding, which continues in a clockwise direction. The first player may pass or bid one of the four suits, as may subsequent players, provided that once a bid has been made, subsequent bids must be of a higher ranked suit than the last. If two players pass consecutively, then the player who bid last wins the contract and becomes the declarer.

If all three players pass, a second round of bidding begins. In this round of bidding, a bidder may again pass or may add a chip or chips to the pot for the privilege of taking the two cards of the talon into his hand in exchange for discarding. If a player adds chips to the pot, a subsequent player may add more. The player who adds most to the pot wins the right to be declarer and to name the trump suit as before, but this time he is allowed to exchange any cards in the talon (none, one or two, according to their value to him) for the same number from his hand. The talon is only used if the bidding goes to a second round. If all players pass on both rounds, the deal is abandoned and passes.

Incidentally, this second round of bidding is the reason the multiplier is necessary in calculating winnings. If a declarer in spades or clubs, say, took out only one or two chips from the pot if successful, he would certainly not pay a chip into the pot merely on the possibility of improving his hand with the talon.

Play
The eldest hand leads to the first trick; see p148 for an explanation of tricks and trick-taking. The play is clockwise. Players must follow suit if possible, and if unable to may trump or discard. A trick is won by the highest trump it contains, otherwise by the highest card in the suit led. The winner of a trick leads to the next.

Play ends when all ten tricks have been played, although once the declarer has made six tricks, or the defenders five, it is not necessary to play out any tricks remaining.

Settlement A successful declarer takes from the pot the number of chips corresponding to the value of the trump suit (hearts four, diamonds three, spades two and clubs one), multiplied by the agreed multiplier, for example five, as suggested. An unsuccessful declarer adds to the pot the number of chips he would have won; for example, had the contract been in hearts, he would add 20.

Example hand
The hands are dealt as shown, using the Bridge convention of calling the players North, East and West (South not being used as this is a three-player game).

North

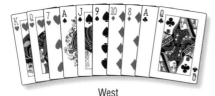

West

East

East is the dealer. West passes, having no long suit. North has a good hand with two long suits, clubs and diamonds. With clubs as trumps, he thinks he should make three tricks in the suit, as there are only three trumps against him. He will probably lose to ♣A and ♣Q, but unless all three missing trumps are in the same hand, he will make three trumps. Unless diamonds are led and trumped, he will almost certainly make three diamonds, too – if each of his opponents holds two diamonds, he will make all four. He knows that East cannot overbid him in spades, as spades is a lower ranking suit than clubs, but he fears that East might overbid in hearts. He is confident enough to bid clubs on the first round, which means he cannot look at the talon, but which also deprives East of the chance of bidding on a second round when he might have use of the talon. As it happens, East has no suit he can bid on any round, so North becomes declarer in clubs.

West has the lead. West knows that he will make two trump tricks when North leads trumps, and he wants to keep a double guard in hearts, in case that is North's second suit. He decides to lead a 'neutral' diamond. The play proceeds:

	West	North	East
1	♦8	♦A	♦7
2	♣A	♣K	♣10
3	♦10	♦K	♦Q
4	♣Q	♣J	♠7
5	♠A	♣7	♠8
6	♠9	♣9	♥10

At this point North will probably show his remaining trump card and his two master diamonds to show that he cannot be stopped from making seven tricks in all. He therefore makes his contract, and as the value of his trump suit was two, and the multiplier is five, he collects ten chips from the pot.

Racing

There are at least two ways in which the Sport of Kings has been refashioned from the green of the turf to that of the card table. The best of them allows betting at different odds on 'horses' with different chances, and therefore most beautifully captures the spirit of racing; it is this version that is given here.

Type	A simple game that simulates a horse race
Alternative names	Horse Race
Players	Three or more
Special requirements	Chips or cash for betting, and pencil and paper to note down the bets

Aim
To back the winning horse in a four-horse race.

Cards
The standard pack of 52 cards is used.

Preparation
The first banker is chosen by means of all the players drawing a card from a spread pack; the drawer of the highest card (Ace high, 2 low) being first banker, with the bank then passing clockwise after each deal.

A minimum and maximum stake should be agreed.

All four Aces are removed from the pack. Any player who wishes to may shuffle the remainder of the pack, but the banker has the option to shuffle last. The player to the banker's right cuts the cards.

The banker sets out the four Aces (the 'horses') in a column, and deals seven cards face up in a row above them. These form the 'rails'. The winning line is an imaginary line drawn from the far end of the seventh card (see illustration opposite). To win, one of the horses must touch the winning line, ie draw level with the final card in the rails (in the illustration, the ♣7).

The number of cards of each suit among the seven cards forming the rails determines the odds against each suit, as represented by the Ace.

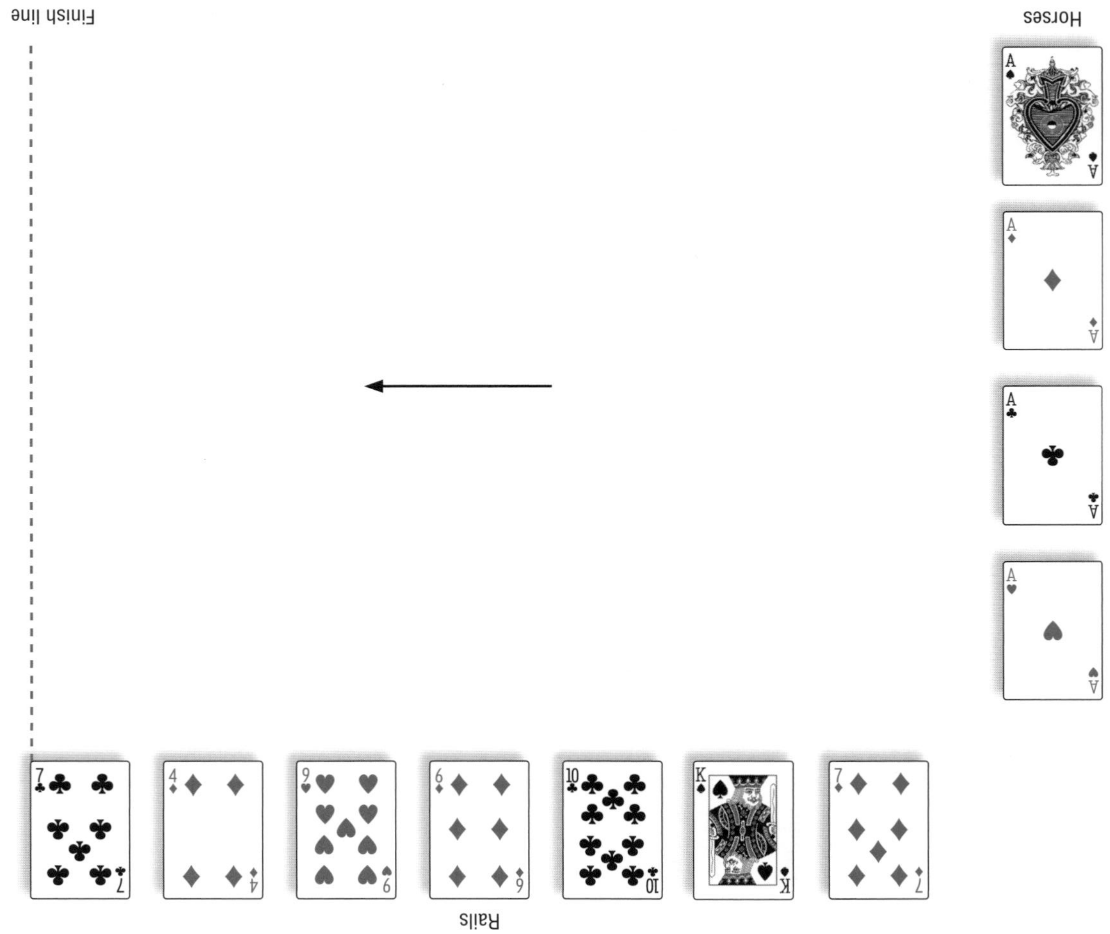

Racing

Rails

Finish line

Horses

Suggested odds are as follows:

Number of cards of a particular suit in the rails	Odds offered against the suit winning
0	5–4
1	2–1
2	3–1
3	6–1
4	12–1
5	50–1
6 or 7	redeal

The odds against each suit in the illustration would therefore be: 2–1 hearts, 2–1 spades, 3–1 clubs, 6–1 diamonds. The odds suggested are slightly in the favour of the banker, so at the end of the game each player should have held the bank an equal number of times.

Players have the option of backing one or more of the suits to win. They pass their chips or money to the banker (who is acting as a bookmaker) and he notes the backer, the amount of the stake and the suit backed.

Play
The banker then turns over the cards in the pack one at a time. If the first card turned is a heart, he moves the ♥A one space towards the winning line, ie in the illustration he moves it horizontally to below ♦7.

He continues to turn up successive cards, each time moving the Ace of the suit turned up one space towards the winning line. When an Ace touches the winning line the race is over, and the banker pays the winnings due to any player who backed the winning suit. The cards (except the Aces) are collected up and the bank passes to the left. It is essential that the cards are well shuffled between each deal.

Variants
Instead of fixing overall limits for the bets, and using the table of odds suggested above, some players prefer to allow the banker to set the limits for betting and also to allow him to quote his own odds on each runner.

Some players prefer that the winning Ace should actually pass the winning line, rather than merely reach it. In this case there must be a redeal if there are five cards or more of one suit in the rails, since that suit would be unable to win, and also the odds table would need to be revised.

Red Dog

Red Dog is a simple gambling game best played among families for pennies rather than taken seriously. The reason is that a serious gambler, prepared to work out his chances on every hand (which can be done quickly), will certainly win in the long run. It is therefore not a game found in casinos. The game is similar to Slippery Sam.

Type	A game involving evaluating a hand
Alternative names	High-card Pool
Players	Three to eight
Special requirements	Chips or cash for staking; a bowl, saucer or similar receptacle for holding the pool

Aim
To win stakes by betting on your hand to beat the turn-up card.

Cards
The standard pack of 52 cards is used, the cards ranking from Ace (high) to 2 (low).

Preparation
A minimum stake must be agreed – if chips are used it would be one chip.

A bowl or saucer is placed in the centre of the table, and a pool is made by all players contributing chips or cash to it. The amount per player will depend upon the number of players: three or four might contribute ten chips each, and seven or eight players might contribute six chips each. It is advised that a maximum stake should be agreed before play begins.

Any player may pick up the cards, shuffle and deal a card to each player. The player dealt the highest card becomes the first dealer. The deal subsequently passes to the left. The dealer may have a hand himself and partake in the game, or, if there are more than four players, it might be preferable for him to deal and collect the cards only. Each player should deal an equal number of times.

The dealer shuffles and the player to his right cuts. The dealer deals five cards face down, one at a time clockwise, to each player beginning with the 'eldest hand' (the player to the dealer's left). The remaining cards are placed face down to form a 'stock'.

Play
The eldest hand examines his cards, and bets that he has a card in his hand of the same suit and of a higher rank than the card on top of the stock. To make a bet, he places the chips he wishes to bet to the side of the bowl containing the pool and announces the amount. Each bet must be of a minimum of one chip. Traditionally,

the maximum bet is the total value of the pool, but it seems sensible that if the game is played among friends or family there should be a maximum of, say, five chips. Otherwise, since good play – play intended to win – suggests that the maximum bet should be made whenever the chances of winning are odds-on, which is often, the pool would be won almost every deal, and as much time could be spent replenishing the pool as in actual play (see Strategy, below).

The dealer then turns over the top card of the stock. If the eldest hand has a card to beat the turn-up, he shows it and takes back his stake from the side of the bowl plus an equal amount from the pool. If he hasn't a card to beat the turn-up, he instead places his chips into the pool. His hand and the turn-up are then placed face down to a waste heap.

The player to the eldest hand's left then makes a bet, similarly placing his chips and announcing the amount, the dealer turns over the next card, and so on.

If the whole pool is won, the players must replenish it by the same amounts as at the beginning.

Strategy The advantage is entirely with the player, since he can bet as little or as much as he wishes. The optimum play would be to bet the maximum whenever there is an odds-on chance of winning and the minimum whenever the chance is odds-against. It is easy to calculate the chances. The player holds five cards and there are 47 unknown (unless some players have played and cards have been exposed, when there will be fewer). So far as the eldest hand is concerned, there are 47 unknown. If he subtracts the rank of the top card he holds in each suit from 14 (counting Aces as 14, Kings as 13, Queens as 12 and Jacks as 11 and a 'void' – not holding any cards in a particular suit – as one) and adds the four figures together, he will know how many cards of the 47 can beat him, and by subtracting that number from 47 how many will not beat him.

Hand A   Hand B

Suppose he holds hand A in the illustration above. Using the method outlined above, his cards count (showing the highest card he holds in each in brackets):

♣ (J)	3
♥ (7)	7
♠ (6)	8
♦ (2)	12
Total	30

There are therefore 30 cards which will beat him and 17 which will not. The odds are against him and, if playing solely to win, he will bet the minimum.

If he held hand B, the cards count:

♣ (Q)	2
♥ (–)	13
♠ (K)	1
♦ (Q)	2
Total	18

There are therefore 18 cards to beat him and 29 which will not. The odds are in his favour, and he should bet the maximum. But this makes for a very boring game and, as stated, it is advised that there is a modest maximum stake.

Variants

Some players give the player a choice of bet: whether he has a card to beat the turn-up, as described, or whether he hasn't. If he bets that he hasn't, he must show his whole hand after the turn-up whether he wins or not. This variant tilts the prospect of winning even more in the player's favour, since he can bet on odds-on chances in every hand he gets.

Schafkopf

Schafkopf, which means 'sheepshead', is the ancestor of the national German game of Skat. The game is over 200 years old, being first mentioned in print in 1811. It has spread around the world, and there are many distinct versions of it in different countries. The description here is a basic version for four players still popular in Germany.

Type	A trick-taking game of skill
Alternative names	None
Players	Four
Special requirements	Chips or cash for staking; a bowl or saucer for holding the pool of stakes

Aim

If playing solo, or on the side holding the 'old women', to win in tricks sufficient point-scoring cards to win the majority of the points (61 or more). If on the other side, to score 60 points.

Cards

The standard pack of 52 cards is used, from which are removed the 6s, 5s, 4s, 3s, and 2s, leaving a pack of 32 cards.

All Queens and Jacks are trumps, as are diamonds, although in some circumstances the trump suit of diamonds can be changed for another. The trump suit ranks ♣Q, ♠Q, ♥Q, ♦Q, ♣J, ♠J, ♥J, ♦J, A, 10, K, 9, 8, 7. The two black Queens, as the top trumps, are known as the 'old women' (*die Alten*).

In the plain suits the cards rank A, 10, K, 9, 8, 7.

Preparation

The value of the staking unit or the chip, if chips are to be used, has to be agreed.

The dealer is decided by any acceptable method, such as any player picking up the cards, shuffling and beginning to deal cards one at a time to each player round the table until a Jack appears. The player dealt the Jack becomes the first dealer.

The dealer shuffles, the player to his right cuts, and the dealer deals eight cards to each player in two bundles of four, clockwise beginning with the 'eldest hand' (the player to his left).

The game is usually played for stakes, and a pool is formed. A convenient number of chips for each player to contribute to a pool is 50, making a pool of 200.

Play

Each player plays for himself, but in each hand there are likely to be temporary partners, as the two players dealt the old women (♣Q and ♠Q) play as partners against the other two. They do not identify themselves, so no player knows who his partner is until it becomes clear during the play.

A player dealt both old women has the choice of playing solo or calling for a partner. His options are:

i)   To call for a partner by naming any card he does not hold. The player who holds the card becomes the partner but does not identify himself.

ii) To play solo in secret. His opponents will not know he is playing solo.

iii) To declare before play starts that he is playing solo. This gives him the opportunity to change the trump suit from diamonds to whatever he wishes. He must, of course, announce the trump suit when making his declaration. The Queens and Jacks remain trumps in their usual order, but are followed as trumps by A, 10, K, 9, 8, 7 of the named suit.

A player dealt only one of the old women also has the chance of playing solo. He has two options if he wants to play solo:

i)   To play solo in secret. As soon as the other black Queen is played, he must declare he is playing solo, so that the holder of the other black Queen knows he is an opponent of the declarer and not his partner.

ii) To declare he is playing solo before play starts, which gives him the opportunity to change the trump suit as described above.

It is necessary to hold a black Queen to play solo. A player playing solo against the other three players must still score 61 or more points to win.

Players examine their hands, during which time a player wishing to declare solo must do so. The 'eldest hand' (the player to the dealer's left) then leads to the first trick; see p148 for an explanation of tricks and trick-taking. Normal trick-taking rules apply, ie players must follow suit to the card led if they can (bearing in mind that all Queens and Jacks are trumps and not therefore part of a plain suit), and if they cannot they may trump or discard. When a trump is led, all players must follow with a trump if they can. A trick is won by the highest trump it contains if any, and if not by the highest card in the suit led. The winner of a trick leads to the next.

Settlement Some cards have a value when captured in tricks, as follows:

Ace	11 points	King	4 points
10	10 points	Queen	3 points

Jack	2 points

The other cards have no scoring value. Hence, there are 120 points in the whole pack to be won.

If the players holding the old women win (ie score 61 or more points), they each take chips from the pool as follows:

61–89 points	5 chips
90–120 points (known as *schneider*)	10 chips
winning all ten tricks (known as *schwarz*)	15 chips

If the players holding the old women lose (ie fail to score 61 or more points), their opponents take from the pool as follows:

60–89 points	10 chips
90+ points (*schneider*)	20 chips

When players go solo, they settle individually without recourse to the pool. A soloist who wins receives five chips from each opponent for 61–89 points, ten chips from each for schneider and 15 for schwarz. If he loses, he pays double these amounts.

Example hand

The hands are dealt as shown, using the Bridge convention of calling players North, South, East and West. West is the dealer.

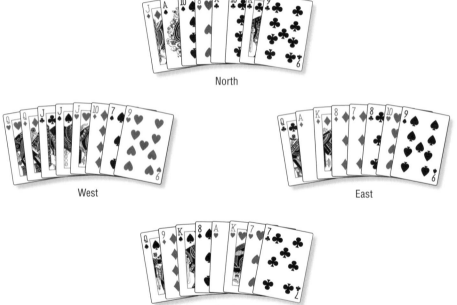

Neither East nor South, the holders of the old women, have a hand with which they could possibly go solo. North, who has the opening lead, decides that as he is strong in the black plain suits, he will lead a trump in the hope of clearing enough trumps to make some plain suit winners, a policy which could go wrong. Play proceeds:

	North	East	South	West
1	♦ J	♦ A	♠ Q	♥ J

East, presuming North did not hold ♠Q, played ♦A to allow his partner, whoever it might be, to win it with ♠Q. He would prefer the holder of the ♠Q to be West, because West could win the trick, containing 13 points already, with as small a trump as necessary. However, it is South who holds ♠Q, and he can see little choice but to win the trick. West played his lowest valued trump on it. South is now stuck for a lead. He tries ♥A, hoping all will follow suit and so collect eleven points for it. It does well as East puts ♥10 on it. All now know that East and South are partners, and already have 39 points, but things go wrong for East and South from trick 3, when South, rather than lead his only trump, leads his bare club:

2	♥8	♥10	<u>♥A</u>	♥9
3	<u>♣A</u>	♣8	♣7	♠7
4	♠A	♠9	♠8	♦10

From trick 4, West holds nothing but trumps. He knows the only trick he can now lose is to East's ♣Q. East does as well as possible by taking North's ♠10, and hopes that South can play ♣10 upon the same trick, which would win the game for East and South, but unfortunately North holds ♣10.

5	♣9	♦7	♦9	♠J
6	♣K	♦8	♥7	<u>♥Q</u>
7	♠10	<u>♣Q</u>	♥K	♣J
8	♣10	♦K	♠K	<u>♦Q</u>

So East/South scored 58 points, despite holding the old women, and North/West made 62. North and West each take ten chips from the pool.

Slippery Sam

Slippery Sam is a very simple gambling game which is almost the same game as Red Dog. It favours the players against the bank, so to be fair all players must hold the bank an equal number of times.

Type	A banking game
Alternative names	Shoot
Players	Three to ten; five or six is best
Special requirements	Chips or cash for staking

Aim

To hold a card of the same suit but higher rank than the banker's card, and to win by betting accordingly.

Cards

The standard pack of 52 cards is used, the cards ranking from Ace (high) to 2 (low).

Preparation

The minimum unit of stake must be agreed; if chips are used the value of the chip must be agreed.

Any player may pick up the cards, shuffle and begin to deal cards one at a time to each player round the table until a Jack appears. The player dealt the Jack becomes the first dealer, and consequently the banker. The deal subsequently passes to the left.

The banker must put chips into a pool to a fixed amount, to be agreed beforehand. He shuffles the cards and the player to his right cuts. Starting with the player to his left, he then deals the cards face down, one at a time, clockwise to all players, until each player has three cards. He then places the remainder of the pack face down in front of him to form the 'stock'.

Since Slippery Sam is a banking game, it must be agreed beforehand that each player will hold the bank for an agreed number of hands (three is suggested), after which time he may withdraw any chips remaining in the bank. A minimum stake should also be agreed.

Play

The banker deals with each player in turn, beginning with the player to his left. After studying his cards, this player must bet an amount, between the minimum agreed stake and the whole of the bank, that he has a card in his hand of the same suit but a higher rank than the card on top of the stock. He advances his stake halfway towards the bank in the centre and announces its amount.

The banker then exposes the top card of the stock. If the player has in his hand a higher card in that suit, he shows it and withdraws his stake plus an equal amount from the bank. If the player cannot beat the exposed card, he puts his stake into the bank. In either case, the banker takes the four cards (the hand and the exposed card from stock), and keeps them in a face-down waste pile beside him. No player may look at the cards in this pile.

If anything in the bank remains, the banker deals with the next player in turn in the same manner. No player may look at his cards until it is his turn to bet.

It is customary for a player who wishes to bet the whole amount of the bank on his hand to say 'shoot'. If he wins he takes the whole bank, that deal ends, and the player to the banker's left becomes the new banker and must put up the agreed amount to the new bank.

A banker holds the bank for the agreed number of rounds, but because the odds are stacked in favour of the player, it is unlikely that the bank will survive for the full number of rounds (for example, three). If it does, the banker withdraws any chips or currency remaining and the next player becomes banker.

Between each round the cards, including the discards, are shuffled and cut again.

Strategy As with Red Dog, it is easy to calculate the chances of any hand winning. The highest card in each suit is deducted from 14 (Aces count 14, Kings 13, Queens 12 and Jacks 11, and other cards at their face value). The totals are added and 13 is added for each void suit. The overall total is the number of cards in the stock (or dealt elsewhere) that will beat the hand. As there are 49 unknown cards, the number subtracted from 49 will give the number of cards that will not beat the hand. The illustration shows how it works.

Hand A   Hand B

Hand A has no cards that will beat it in spades, one in diamonds, four in clubs and thirteen in hearts. This makes 18 cards to beat it and 31 which will lose, or odds on winning of approximately 5–3. Hand B's figures are 43–6 or approximately 7–1 against winning. As a player with a better than even chance of beating the up-turned card from the stock will usually shoot (and win), the banker's best policy is to regard the money he puts into the bank as lost (or to regard it as a bonus if he takes some of his bank back) and to rely on winning when it is his turn to be a player.

Variants

To give the banker a better chance of withdrawing some chips when his turn as banker ends, some players prefer that each banker holds the bank for one deal only.

Some players prefer that the players do not look at their hands. The banker exposes his card and players make their bets and then look at their hands to see if they've won. This gives the banker a better chance. If his turn-up is an Ace, he cannot lose, and all players will bet the minimum. If his turn-up is a 2, the odds are about 5–4 in favour of the player. The odds are at their closest when the banker's card is a 4; above 4 the odds favour the banker, below 4 the players.

Solo Whist

Solo Whist came to Britain in the 19th century, and seems to have more roots in Ombre than Whist itself, with which it developed a rivalry in the late 19th century until Bridge submerged both. Solo, as it is usually called, still flourishes as a game in pubs, canteens, railway carriages and family social evenings, being one of those widely played games where local rules apply. It is usually played for small stakes.

Type	A trick-taking game
Alternative names	None
Players	Four
Special requirements	Chips or cash for staking

Aim
To win the contract through bidding and thereafter to make the number of tricks required by the contract. Otherwise, as a defender, to defeat the soloist's contract.

Cards
The standard pack of 52 cards is used, the cards ranking from Ace (high) to 2 (low).

Preparation
The basic stake must be agreed.

Players draw cards from a spread pack to determine the first dealer. The drawer of the highest card deals. The deal subsequently passes to the left.

The cards are shuffled by the dealer before the first deal and cut by the player to his right. After the first deal, however, the cards are not shuffled, merely collected up and the pack cut. The dealer deals the cards in four bundles of three cards to each player, the last four cards being dealt singly. The last one of all (the dealer's) is turned face up to indicate the trump suit (it might be changed later).

Bidding Beginning with the 'eldest hand' (the player to the dealer's left), each player may make a bid or pass. Each bid must be higher than a previous bid, except when accepting a proposal (see below). A player may not bid after he has passed, with the exception of the eldest hand, who may accept a proposal. The bidding ends after three consecutive passes, with the last bidder becoming the soloist. The possible bids, in ascending order, are:

Proposal   A player who states 'I propose' is asking for a partner with whom he can make eight tricks playing against the other two players, with the turn-up as trumps. Unless there is an intervening bid, any player can accept the proposal by saying 'I accept'. In practice, the popular terms usually used for 'I propose' and 'I accept' are 'prop' and 'cop'. If no other player makes a bid, the two players become 'joint soloists'. They do not change seats to sit opposite each other. If the eldest hand has passed, and another player proposes, the eldest hand is not barred, because he passed, from accepting the proposal. The eldest hand has another privilege. If he proposes, and all others pass, he may upgrade his bid to one of solo, if he wishes.

Solo	An undertaking to make five tricks with the turn-up suit as trumps.
Misère	An undertaking to lose all the tricks. This contract is played without a trump suit. The popular term is 'mis'.
Abundance	An undertaking to win nine tricks with the declarer naming the trump suit.
Royal abundance	An undertaking to win nine tricks with the turn-up suit as trumps. This bid is not necessary (just abundance would suffice) unless a previous bidder has bid abundance. A bid of royal abundance takes precedence, although the rewards are the same.
Misère ouvert (open misère)	An undertaking not to win any tricks, with the hand exposed on the table for opponents to see after the first trick has been played. The contract is played with no trumps. Opponents see the exposed hand but are not allowed to discuss ways of defeating it.
Abundance declared	An undertaking to win all 13 tricks, the declarer naming the trump suit.

If all players pass, the sorted hands are collected up without them being shuffled. The combined pack is then cut and the next player deals. This is called a 'goulash' deal and leads to freak hands.

Play

If the contract is abundance or abundance declared, the soloist names the trump suit. The eldest hand leads to the first trick, unless the contract is abundance declared, when the soloist leads. If the contract is misère ouvert, the soloist lays his cards on the table after the first trick has been played.

The usual rules of trick-taking apply; see p148 for an explanation of tricks and trick-taking. Players must follow suit to the card led if able, and if they cannot may trump or discard. A trick is won by the highest trump it contains, or if it contains none by the highest card in the suit led. The winner of a trick leads to the next.

Settlement Settlement is made after each hand, with the soloist, if successful, winning from each opponent according to the following scale:

Proposal and acceptance	2 units	Abundance	4 units
Solo	2 units	Misère ouvert	6 units
Misère	3 units	Abundance declared	8 units

If he fails he pays each player on the same scale.

Note that in proposal and acceptance, each winning partner receives two units from one of the two defenders, so the profit is two units per player. In solo, which apparently has the same tariff, the winner receives six units (two from each opponent) or loses six, so solo has a higher tariff than proposal and acceptance.

Strategy Solo and abundance contracts normally rely on the distribution of the cards – it is difficult to squeeze extra tricks by skill. The most interesting bid is misère, and skill can play a part here. One thing to be avoided is to bid misère with a long suit lacking the 2. Opponents can discover the weakness and discard in that suit until they hold the 2 only, which can defeat the contract.

Example hand
The hands are dealt as shown, using the Bridge convention of calling the players North, South, East and West.

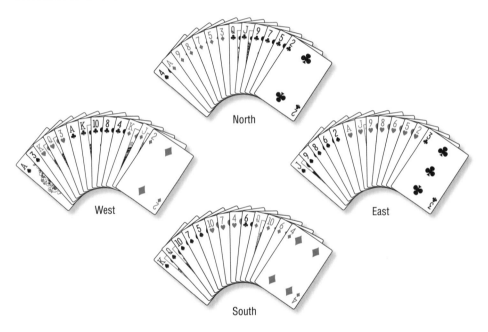

Both North and East's hands would be considered freakish in Bridge, but they are typical of Solo, where the cards are not shuffled between hands. South dealt and the last card he was dealt was ♣6, which makes clubs trumps.

West bids first and bids solo, expecting to make two or three trumps, a spade and one or two tricks in the red suits. North bids misère, which somewhat surprises East, who was going to bid misère himself. East decides not to bid misère ouvert, fearing his spade suit might be vulnerable if his cards were laid down. East and South pass, and North becomes soloist in misère. West decides to lead ♠A, then ♠3 (a ploy which would have sunk East on the third trick had East been allowed to play misère). However, when North played ♠4 (presumably his highest spade) on the Ace, West decided there was no future in spades and decided to repeat his tactics in diamonds.

The play went as follows:

	West	North	East	South
1	♠A	♠4	♠J	♠K
2	♦K	♦9	♥J	♦Q
3	♦J	♦8	♥9	♦10
4	♦2	♦3	♥8	♦6
5	♥K			♦4

North was sunk. West and East were out of diamonds, and North was unable to get below South's lead of ♦4. It was excellent play by West. Most Solo players would have called misère with the North or East hands, and would have failed.

Variants

Common variants are:

i)   Many players prefer the cards to be dealt in four bundles, of four, three, three and three cards.

ii)   Many players ignore the 'prop and cop' bid, on the grounds that it rarely fails and is boring.

iii)   Exposing the dealer's last card to indicate the trump suit is not liked by many and should it be an Ace, say, it affects the game too much. The most popular method of avoiding it is to choose trumps by rote: for example hearts, clubs, diamonds, spades. Each player deals the same trumps every deal, so it is an easy system to operate.

iv)   When the contract is abundance, many players prefer that the first trick is played with the original suit as trumps, with the soloist naming his trump suit before the second trick. Many soloists in abundance have so many trumps that another player is void. If the player who leads can guess the trump suit and lead it, and another player can trump it with the original trump suit, then the soloist is deprived of a trick. It adds an extra angle to the call of abundance and is recommended.

v)   Some players do not like the artificially created freak hands which often result from goulash deals, and prefer a light shuffle.

Auction Solo Auction Solo is played like Solo, but there is a greater variety of bids. This makes the game more interesting, as a drawback of Solo is that there are no positive bids between solo, which is often a laydown, and abundance. Many hands fall between a certain solo and one trick short of abundance.

Auction Solo drops the proposal and acceptance bid. Bidders can bid to make any number of tricks over five. Bids to make five to eight tricks are all called solos (solo of five, solo of six etc). In each a player can choose his trump suit, but a bid of a certain number in the designated trump suit ranks higher than a bid of the same number in the bidder's own suit (as royal abundance overcalls abundance in the game described). A player bidding solo of seven in the trump suit of his choice will bid merely 'solo of seven', which could be overcalled by 'solo of seven in trump suit'.

Misère ranks above solo of eight in trump suit and below an abundance of nine.

Contracts of nine to twelve are called abundances, and again abundance in the trump suit overcalls an abundance of the same number in the bidder's own suit.

After abundance of twelve in the trump suit is ranked misère ouvert, and after that comes abundance declared and abundance declared in the trump suit. Only in abundance declared in his own suit does the soloist have the advantage of the lead. In all other contracts the eldest hand leads.

Settlement to be received from each opponent if successful, and to be paid to each if unsuccessful, is as follows:

Solo	2 units, plus one for each overtrick or undertrick
Misère	4 units
Abundance	6 units, plus one for each overtrick or undertrick
Misère ouvert	8 units
Abundance declared	12 units, plus one for each undertrick

The rewards or penalties for solo and abundance contracts do not change with the number of tricks contracted for. Overtricks and undertricks are based on the number of tricks contracted.

A soloist would be advised to get the contract at as low a level as possible, to maximize overtricks or minimize undertricks, but of course bidding six, say, and getting overbid, means then bidding eight to get the contract when it might have been had for seven.

Spinado

Spinado, or Spin, is a simplified form of the old game Pope Joan, but the name is frequently applied to any of the games of the family, such as Newmarket. Spinado retains the Pope Joan features of 'matrimony' and 'intrigue'.

Type	A game of the Stops family
Alternative names	Spin
Players	Two to seven; four or five is best
Special requirements	Chips or cash for staking; three saucers to hold stakes

Aim
To win stakes by getting rid of all your cards first, and by playing certain bonus cards.

Cards
The standard pack of 52 cards is used, from which are removed the ♦8 and all the 2s, leaving a pack of 47 cards. Cards rank from King (high) to Ace (low).

Preparation
The basic stake should be agreed, eg if chips are to be used, the value of one chip.

Three saucers need to be labelled with the words 'matrimony', 'intrigue' and 'game', and placed in the centre of the table.

Any player may pick up the cards, shuffle and begin to deal cards one at a time to each player round the table until a Jack appears. The player dealt the Jack becomes the first dealer. The deal subsequently passes to the left.

It should be agreed that the game will not end until all players have dealt an equal number of times. On each deal, the dealer contributes twelve chips to the matrimony pool, and six to each of the other two pools. The other players each contribute three chips to the game pool.

The dealer shuffles and the player to his right cuts. The dealer deals the cards one at a time clockwise, face down, to each player including himself and also to a 'widow' which is the first hand to his left. The widow is placed to one side face down and not used. Players are dealt an equal number of cards, with any remainder being added to the widow. Players and widow therefore receive cards as follows:

Number of players	Cards received	Widow	Number of players	Cards received	Widow
2	15	17	5	7	12
3	11	14	6	6	11
4	9	11	7	5	12

Play

The 'eldest hand' (the player to the dealer's left) begins by playing any card he likes to the table before him, announcing its rank and suit. The player with the next highest card in the suit then plays it, announcing its rank (the suit needs to be announced only at the beginning of the sequence). The player with the next highest card in the suit then plays that, and so on. Players may play two or more cards at once if they hold a sequence.

Eventually the run will come to a stop, because the sequence reaches a King, or because the next card required is not available. A card is unavailable either because it has been withdrawn (ie the ♦8 and the four 2s), or because it is in the widow. The player who played the last card before a stop then begins a new sequence by playing any card from his hand.

During the game, stakes are won from other players by playing certain cards. One of them is ♦A, known as 'spinado' or 'spin'. A player who plays it collects three chips from each of the other players. A player can play spinado at any time that he is playing a legitimate card, for example if the sequence reaches ♠8 and the holder of spinado holds ♠9, he can play ♠9 and add ♦A, announcing 'nine and spin'. Spinado is a stop so, after collecting from the opponents, the player of spinado begins a new sequence by playing a card of his choice.

Spinado   Marriage   Intrigue

The special cards in Spinado

During the game, a player who plays both ♦J and ♦Q claims 'intrigue', and picks up the chips in the saucer so marked. A player who plays both ♦Q and ♦K picks up the chips in the 'matrimony' saucer. If a player is lucky enough to hold and play ♦J, Q, K he picks up the chips in both saucers.

A player who plays ♦K, whether he also collects for matrimony or not, receives two chips from each of the other players. The players of any of the other three kings collect one chip from the others.

A player who gets rid of all his cards takes the stakes in the 'game' saucer. He also collects one chip from the other players for each card remaining in their hands, and two chips per card from a player unlucky enough to be caught with spinado in his hand. The winner of the game is also exempt from putting a stake into the game pool for the next deal, unless he happens to be the dealer, who must always put the requisite amounts into the three saucers.

More often than not, the matrimony and intrigue pools are not collected during the hand. The stakes in them remain for the next deal, and since their saucers are added to with each deal, the stakes contained in them can rise to large amounts.

Strategy Players should be aware of the stop cards, which are the Kings, the Aces, ♦7 and any card immediately below a card which has already been used to begin a sequence. For example, if ♣J has been played, the holder of ♣10 knows it is a stop card and that he can play it with impunity. Players with cards which carry a bonus, such as spinado, Kings, matrimony or intrigue will usually play them at the first opportunity in case the chance never comes again. This is not always best play, but is sound if there are many players holding small hands; for example, with seven players holding five cards each (and twelve in the widow) a player may not get a chance to play a card, let alone two chances, so holding up a bonus card could be fatal.

Spoil Five

Spoil Five is one of those ancient trick-taking games of the Euchre, Écarté and Napoleon family, in which the hand consists of five cards and the ranking of the cards is eccentric. Spoil Five is the version which gained popularity in Ireland, and is, or was, frequently referred to as the national card game of Ireland. It borrows from the Spanish game of Ombre, and under an old name, Maw, was the favourite of James VI of Scotland (James I of England).

Type	A trick-taking game
Alternative names	Maw, Twenty-Five
Players	Two to ten; five or six is best
Special requirements	Chips or cash for staking; a bowl or saucer for holding the pool of stakes

Aim
To win three of the five tricks in each deal, or to win all five; if neither is possible, to prevent another player from doing so.

Cards
The standard pack of 52 cards is used. The ranking of the cards differs according to which suit is trumps. The highest trump is always the 5, followed by the Jack. The third trump is always ♥A, no matter which suit is trumps. The rank of the cards in a trump suit is as follows:

hearts	5 (high), J, A, K, Q, 10, 9, 8, 7, 6, 4, 3, 2
diamonds	5 (high), J, ♥A, A, K, Q, 10, 9, 8, 7, 6, 4, 3, 2
clubs	5 (high), J, ♥A, A, K, Q, 2, 3, 4, 6, 7, 8, 9, 10
spades	5 (high), J, ♥A, A, K, Q, 2, 3, 4, 6, 7, 8, 9, 10

The rank of the cards in a plain suit is as follows:

hearts	K (high), Q, J, 10, 9, 8, 7, 6, 5, 4, 3, 2
diamonds	K (high), Q, J, 10, 9, 8, 7, 6, 5, 4, 3, 2, A
clubs	K (high), Q, J, A, 2, 3, 4, 5, 6, 7, 8, 9, 10
spades	K (high), Q, J, A, 2, 3, 4, 5, 6, 7, 8, 9, 10

Notice that the rank of the cards below the court cards is reversed in the black suits, expressed by 'highest in red, lowest in black'. Aces rank above the court cards when trumps, and below when in plain suits.

Preparation

The basic stake should be agreed, eg if chips are to be used, the value of one chip.

Each player puts one chip into a saucer placed in the middle of the table, forming the pool.

Any player may pick up the cards, shuffle and begin to deal cards one at a time to each player round the table until a Jack appears. The player dealt the Jack becomes the first dealer. The deal passes to the left, and the game should not end until all players have dealt an equal number of times.

Beginning with the 'eldest hand' (the player to the dealer's left), and dealing clockwise, the dealer deals five cards to each player, in bundles of three and two, or two and three, whichever he prefers. The dealer places the remainder of the cards face down on the table and turns up the top card to indicate the trump suit.

Robbing the trump Unless the turn-up is an Ace, any player who holds the Ace of trumps must announce it before he plays to the first trick. If he fails to do this, the Ace is demoted to be the lowest trump in that deal. Announcing the Ace allows him to take the up-card into his hand by passing a discard face down to the dealer, who places it unseen under the pack and hands the player the turn-up. The player receiving the turn-up does not have to play it, or the Ace, on that trick. If the holder of the Ace does not want the turn-up, he announces his Ace but tells the dealer to 'turn it down', whereupon the dealer turns the card over.

If the turn-up is an Ace, the dealer is allowed to exchange a card for it. To do so, he must discard any card face down before a card is led, although it is customary that he leaves the Ace on the pack until it is his turn to play, when he takes it into his hand. If the dealer has not discarded when the eldest hand wants to lead to the first trick, the eldest hand must call upon the dealer to do so. In the unlikely event that the dealer does not wish to take the card, the dealer says 'I play with these', and play begins.

Play

The eldest hand makes the first lead; see p148 for an explanation of tricks and trick-taking. Trick-taking rules are unusual. A player who can follow suit must do so or trump, ie he may trump even though he can follow suit. A player who cannot follow suit may play any card. Players must follow suit if able when a trump is led, except when 'reneging' (see below).

A trick is won by the highest trump it contains, otherwise by the highest card in the suit led. The winner of a trick leads to the next.

Reneging A privilege attaches to the three highest trumps, ie to the 5, J and ♥A. They cannot be forced out by the lead of a smaller trump. If a small trump is led, a player is not forced to follow with one of these trumps, and if he has no smaller trumps he may discard. This is called 'reneging'. The lead of a superior trump, however, calls for the play of an inferior trump, ie if the trump 5 is led, a player must follow with J or ♥A if he holds no other trump.

Each player plays for himself, with his main object to win three tricks, which entitles him to the pool. If a player cannot win three tricks, he tries to prevent any other player doing so. If nobody wins three tricks, the hand is 'spoiled', hence the name of the game, and the pool is carried forward to the next deal. Once a player takes three tricks, the rest of the hand is not played, unless the tricks won are the first three.

The winner of them may throw in his remaining cards and take the pool, or he may 'jink it'. This is an announcement that he proposes to take the last two tricks as well, for which he not only takes the pool, but is paid a bonus of one chip from each of the other players. If he jinks it and fails, however, he loses his entitlement to the pool and the hand is spoiled.

The deal passes to the left. When a hand is spoiled, the pool remains and only the new dealer adds a chip to it. When the pool is won, all players contribute one chip each to the new pool.

Strategy Most Spoil Five hands are won by a player being dealt a strong hand in trumps (either high ones or length) and leading them out. The majority of hands, with five or more players, are spoiled. Frequently, players see they cannot make three tricks as soon as they see their hands, and concentrate on spoiling other players.

If a player leads three high trumps to win the first three tricks it sometimes pays for a player holding a big trump to renege and allow the winner of the three tricks (who may well hold a fourth) to jink it and attempt to win all five. The hand can then be spoiled.

Example hand
Suppose five hands are dealt by Player A, as illustrated.

Player A   Player B   Player C

Player D   Player E

The turn up was ♦10, which Player E, on his turn, took into his hand, discarding another card, by announcing that he held ♦A before playing to the first trick. The illustration, for convenience, shows Player E with ♦10 already in his hand.

Player B leads to the first trick with prospects of taking three tricks. He bases his hopes on the fact that there are 27 cards not in play. If they include two of ♦5, ♦J and ♦A, Player B hopes that by leading trumps he may win ♥A or ♦K, and later a second trump (which by the third trick might be the only trump left) then he has ♣K to make a third trick. He accordingly leads ♥A and play proceeds:

	Player A	Player B	Player C	Player D	Player E
1	♣6	♥A	♦4	♦2	♦10
2	♠5	♦K	♠9	♠6	♦A

Player D held up ♦5 on the first trick, hoping to make it on the third trick, with the possibility that if ♣K is not in play he could then make ♣Q and ♣7. On the second lead, therefore, he reneged, knowing that Player E held ♦A and that Player B's ♦K would not win the trick.

3	♥5	♦7	♥10	♦5	♥K
4	♠3	♣K	♠8	♣Q	♥8

Having been disappointed that Player D held ♦5 and foiled his plan, Player B now has a second chance by virtue of Player D leading ♣Q. Player B is now very optimistic that ♣3 will win him the game, since only by Player D holding ♣J or ♣A will he be beaten.

5	♥J	♣3	♠J	♣7	♠7

So Player B won his three tricks and collected the pool.

In the example hand, Player B's tactics were correct, but he succeeded only because Player D saw the chance of winning himself. Player D could have prevented Player B from getting his third trick by reneging again when ♦7 was led at trick 3. He could have used ♦5 on Player B's ♣K on trick 4, and then led ♣Q to foil Player B on the last trick. On the other hand, Player B could have given himself a better chance by discarding ♣3 on trick 3 rather than trumping. If another player had reneged by holding up ♦5 or ♦J, hoping to make these tricks himself (as Player D had) that player would have had to have played it on trick 3. Player B would then have held the last trump and the master club for the last two tricks.

Stuss

Stuss is a simplified form of an old game called Faro. Faro was played in France in the time of Louis XIV, when it was called Pharaoh. It became one of the principal gambling games in the casinos of 18th-century England, and in the 19th century it was one of the most popular games played in the gambling houses of the Wild West. To play Faro as it was played in casinos requires particular equipment, such as a special dealing box and a casekeeper resembling an abacus, while Stuss retains the main element of the game and is suitable for home play.

Type	A banking game of chance, with no skill involved
Alternative names	Jewish Faro
Players	Any number above two, with eight to ten best
Special requirements	Chips or cash for betting; the spade suit from a spare set of cards which is used to form a betting layout

Aim
To bet on a rank of card that will appear as a winning card before it appears as a losing card.

Cards
A standard 52-card pack is used.

Preparation
A banker is required. There is an advantage in favour of the bank, so each player should have the chance to hold the bank if he should wish to.

The pack is spread and players who wish to hold the bank draw a card. The player who draws the highest card (Ace high, 2 low) becomes the banker for the first deal. The banker sets the limits for minimum and maximum bets. After the first deal the bank passes to the left, but a player may refuse it if he wishes.

The spades from another pack are set out in the centre of the table to form a betting layout. Traditionally this layout contains two rows of six cards with the odd card (the 7) placed to one side between the rows (see illustration overleaf).

A bet is on a single rank of card only, ie players cannot bet on pairs or any other combination of cards. However, players may make separate single bets on as many cards as they wish provided each bet is within the agreed limits. Any player who wishes may shuffle, but the banker has the option of shuffling last. The player to his right cuts the cards, and the banker takes them into his hand face down.

Play

The banker deals the first card face up to the right of the layout. This card is a losing card for the players, and the banker collects all stakes placed on the rank of the card in the layout.

The banker then deals the second card face up to the left of the layout. This is a winning card for the players, and all who bet on this rank in the layout are paid by the banker at odds of even money, or 1 to 1.

Each pair of cards constitutes a turn. If they are of the same rank the bank wins all bets on that rank, since the losing card is dealt first, and there are therefore no stakes left on that rank when the second card is dealt.

Between turns players may make new bets or add to existing bets. When all are done, the banker turns the next card face up to the right of the layout, placing it on top of the previous card dealt there, thus beginning a losing pile of cards. Similarly, the fourth card turned over is added to the winning pile. With each card turned over the banker takes or pays out according to the stakes placed on the relevant ranks in the layout. Cards dealt to the right are always losing cards for the players, those to the left are winning cards.

There are 24 two-card turns, and the last four cards in the pack are not played. The banker shows these four cards and collects any bets there may be remaining on those ranks in the layout.

The banker's advantage comes from these last four cards and from the fact that when two cards of the same rank appear on one turn (known as a 'split') the banker wins.

Thirty-Five

Thirty-Five is a modern version of an old Italian game, although it requires a full pack rather than the Italian 40-card pack. It is a game in which a degree of judgement is involved, and although largely a game of chance it rewards the astute player.

Type	A game involving a pool and often an auction
Alternative names	Trentacinque
Players	Two to five, with four or five best
Special requirements	Chips or cash for betting; a bowl or saucer to hold the pool of stakes

Aim
To hold cards in one suit whose pip value is 35 or more.

Cards
The standard pack of 52 cards is required. Cards have their pip values, with Ace counting as one, and King, Queen, Jack each as ten.

Preparation
The winner of each hand collects a pool, so the first thing to do is to decide the amount each player must put into the pool before each hand begins. Sometimes the pool is not won and is carried over, and sometimes it is increased, so the initial amount need not be too extravagant.

The first dealer is chosen by spreading the pack, with each player drawing a card, the holder of the highest (Ace high, 2 low) being first dealer. Thereafter the deal passes to the left with each hand. The dealer takes part in the game as a normal player, and there is no advantage to being the dealer. Any player may shuffle, with the dealer having the right to shuffle last. The player to his right cuts the cards.

Play
The dealer deals one card face down to each player, including himself, and one card to a widow for four rounds, and then continues dealing but missing out the widow, until each player has nine cards, and the widow four. The remaining cards are placed to one side and are not used.

Players examine their hands, and any player with a count of 35 or over in one suit announces and shows it. This wins the pool immediately. Should more than one player have a count of 35 or more, the pool is shared between them, irrespective of the actual count. Any indivisible remainder is left in the pool for the next deal.

Should no player claim the pool, bidding begins for the widow.

Beginning with the player on the dealer's left, each player may state an amount he is prepared to pay for the widow. The objective, and hope, of course is to acquire a card or cards in the widow that would take the player's count in one suit to 35 or more. If he acquires the widow and is successful, he does not necessarily win the whole pool – he will take from the pool an amount equal to his bid. If he is unsuccessful, he must add to the pool the amount of his bid. The object, then, is not to acquire the widow for a little as possible, since that would limit the potential winnings. A judgement has to be made based on how confident one is that the widow will provide the required card or cards, and how much one wants to stake on that confidence.

A player who does not wish to bid, throws in his cards. Bidding continues round the table, with each bid, of course, having to be higher than the last, and can go round the table more than once. If two players are confident that the widow will give them a count of 35 or more, the bidding might exceed the amount of the pool. Eventually there will remain one bidder.

The winning bidder adds the widow to his hand. If he can then show a suit with a count of 35 or more he takes from the pool the amount of his bid. If the bid was for an amount higher than the pool, he takes the whole pool, but cannot claim any excess. If he fails to show a count of 35 he puts in the full amount of his bid (even if it were higher than the pool).

Whether the pool is won or not, the usual amount is put into the pool before the next deal. Some players like to set a limit to the pool, which can grow large. If it exceeds the limit, the excess is shared between the players.

Example game

Player A   Player B

Widow   Player C

Suppose three players receive the hands in the illustration. There are 15 chips in the pool. No player is dealt a hand with a suit counting 35. Player A is first to bid and has a spade suit counting 32. Any two spades in the widow, or any single spade except Ace or 2, would give him a count of 35. He considers it worth a bid and bids six chips. Player B has no prospects whatsoever and throws his hand in. Player C has two suits that might reach 35; hearts with 30 and clubs with 29. Any heart or club higher than a 5 would give him a count of 35. He is willing to bet more than six chips on his chance. He bids ten chips. Player A ups his bid to 12 chips (it is difficult to throw in a hand with a count of 32). Player C increases his bid to 15 chips. Player A does not think (rightly or wrongly) that he has an odds-on chance of getting a spade in the widow, and if he bids more than 15 chips he stands to lose more than he stands to win, so he lets Player C buy the widow. The widow was ♥4, ♣A, ♠6, ♠7. Player C has a heart suit counting 34, and a club suit counting 30, so he loses and must put 15 chips into the pool. As it turns out, Player A would have won the pool had he continued to bid and won the auction.

Thirty-One

Thirty-One is a number that often crops up in gambling games (eg Trente et Quarante, still played in casinos), but the game now known as Thirty-One is usually a watered-down version of the game described below designed for younger players. The gambling version is played for a pool.

Type	A card-counting game rewarding good judgement
Alternative names	Schnautz, Trente-et-Un
Players	Three to 15 (the more the better)
Special requirements	Chips or cash for betting, a bowl or saucer to hold the pool of stakes

Aim
To hold or build a hand of three cards of the same suit with a higher point count than the hands of other players.

Cards
The standard pack of 52 cards is used. Aces count eleven points, court cards ten points and other cards their pip value. If necessary to break a tie, Ace, King, Queen, Jack rank in that order.

Preparation
Before each deal the amount to be put into the pool by all players must be agreed. The first dealer is decided by each player drawing a card from a spread pack; the highest drawer (Ace high, 2 low) becoming first dealer. The deal passes to the left after each deal. The dealer takes part as a normal player, there being no advantage to the dealer in the game. In fact there is a slight disadvantage, as he is last to draw from the widow. Therefore the game should not end before all players have dealt an equal number of times.

The cards are shuffled (the dealer having the right to shuffle last) and the player to the right of the dealer cuts.

Play
The dealer deals cards clockwise one at a time face down to each player beginning with 'eldest' (the player to his left) and one face up to a widow in the centre of the table, until each player and the widow has three cards.

Each player examines his cards and announces it immediately if he holds one of three combinations:

a)   Three cards of one suit with a points count of 31 (this can be only an Ace with any two cards from the four ranks which count ten (K, Q, J, 10). He announces '31 points'.

b) Any three cards of the same rank. This hand is valued at 30½ points, so beats any hand except (a) above. He announces 'three cards'.

c) Three cards of one suit not totalling 31 points, but which he thinks has a points total sufficient to win, ie a higher points total than any other player. He announces his points total.

When a player announces immediately, there is no further play. All players expose their hands and the highest hand wins the pool. Where there is a tie, the hand holding the highest ranking card wins, the cards ranking Ace, King, Queen, Jack,......2. If equal, the next highest card decides and if again equal, the third, and so on. Only if two or more hands are identical is the pool shared.

When no player announces immediately, an exchange of cards begins. Beginning with eldest, each player must exchange one card with the widow. Play continues like this for as many rounds as necessary and a player may, if he wishes, take from the widow a card he previously discarded.

Play continues, with each player trying to improve his hand, of course, until a player has 31 points or is satisfied with his hand. If he has 31 he must announce it immediately. He cannot be beaten and he takes the pool.

If a player has a count he is satisfied with, on his next turn he knocks on the table rather than exchanging a card with the widow (note he cannot knock on the same turn as he exchanges a card). When a player knocks, play continues once round the table until it reaches the knocker. On this last round, players are not forced to exchange a card with the widow – they are allowed to pass.

When the turn reaches the knocker, all players then expose their hands, and the player with the highest count in one suit wins the pool.

Since a player cannot knock without having three cards of the same suit or the same rank, it can happen that the game continues too long without anybody knocking. It is suggested that if there are ten rounds of players exchanging a card without anybody knocking, the hand should be abandoned. The pool remains, the deal passes as usual, and players contribute to the pool as usual, so that the next game has a double pool.

Strategy
Players with any count (ie players with three cards of the same suit) should always consider the possibility of knocking. A count of 25 or so often wins, particularly if dealt initially, when no players have had a chance to exchange cards with the widow. When several rounds of exchanges have been made and the cards in the widow are of low denomination, an even lower count might be worth knocking with – certainly a better option than allowing the hand to be abandoned.

Trente et Quarante

Trente et Quarante is a very old game, possibly well over 300 years old. It was a popular casino game of the heyday of the plush European casinos of the late 19th and early 20th centuries, but began to decline as the glamorous, privileged lifestyle of that time faded; it never crossed the Atlantic to the more vulgar casinos of Las Vegas.

It is a game of no skill whatever.

Type	A game of chance played in casinos
Alternative names	Rouge et Noir
Players	Any number
Special requirements	Played in a casino, which provides the venue, table, cards and chips

Aim
To place winning bets on certain outcomes of chance, ie the relative pip counts of two rows of cards and the colour of a certain card.

Cards
Normally six standard packs of 52 cards are used, shuffled together. Cards have their pip value, with court cards counting ten and Aces one.

Preparation
Players bet by placing their stakes upon the table. The table is double-ended: only half is illustrated.

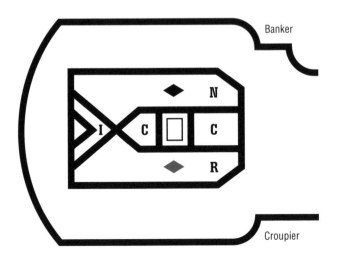

Play

A dealer deals, one at a time face up, a row of cards from the pack and stops when the total value of the cards exceeds 30 (ie when it reaches 31–40). He announces the total. This row represents *noir*, or black. He then deals a second row below it until this row also exceeds 30. He announces this total. This row represents *rouge*, or red. An example of the two rows is shown below. The winning row is that nearer to 31, ie the lower count of the two. In the illustration below, rouge wins. Gamblers who bet on rouge, by placing their stakes on the part of the table marked with R and the red diamond, win the amount of their stake. The bettors on noir (N and the black diamond) lose.

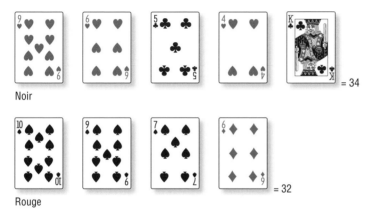

Noir

Rouge

There is another bet the gamblers can make. They can bet that the first card turned up (in the illustration ♥9) will be the same colour as the winning row. This is a bet on *couleur*, and a gambler wishing to bet on couleur places his stakes in the spaces marked C on the table. A bet is also possible on 'inverse', which is a bet that the colour of the first card turned will be the opposite colour to that of the winning row. These bets are placed on the small space on the table marked I.

When the banker completes the second row of cards, and has announced the total, he announces the two winning bets. If he dealt the cards in the illustration, he would announce 'rouge, couleur'.

If the two rows of numbers are equal, the bets are void and gamblers retain their stakes. They can either ask the croupier for their return or leave them for the next rows of cards to be dealt.

All bets are settled at odds of 1–1, or evens. However, since the casino is there to make a profit, there is one occasion when it does so. This is when both rows of cards tie at 31. This is known as a *refait*. When it occurs, the casino claims half of all the stakes. The croupier will return half the stake to each player, or if the player prefers, he may leave the whole stake 'in prison' on the table for the next coup, getting it back if his bet wins or losing the whole stake if it doesn't.

The refait represents the house edge. A tie at 31–31 is estimated to happen roughly once in 40 coups, and it gives the casino an edge of 1.28%. This is one of the smallest of advantages in casino games. A player can reduce it to 1% by insuring against a refait. By purchase of a special chip of 1% of his stake, he does not lose half his stake when refait occurs.

More About Playing Cards

Card Games Basics 147

Card Games Glossary 150

Customs, Practices and Etiquette 157

Card Sharp's Guide 159

Card Games Basics

There are certain basic facts, rules and customs which apply to all card games.

The pack
The standard pack consists of 52 cards containing four suits, each identified by a symbol: spades (♠), hearts (♥), diamonds (♦) and clubs (♣). Hearts and diamonds are printed in red, spades and clubs in black. There are 13 cards in each suit, each having a rank: Ace (A), King (K), Queen (Q), Jack (J), 10, 9, 8, 7, 6, 5, 4, 3, 2. When buying a pack, it is usual to find two additional cards called Jokers, often illustrated with a figure dressed as a court jester, with cap and bells. The Jokers are rarely used but have been added to the pack specially for a few games.

Some games require two or more packs, and some, particularly games which originate from Spain, Italy, Germany or Switzerland, require a 'short pack', which is formed from the standard pack by removing the lower ranking cards: for a 40-card pack, the 4s, 3s and 2s are removed; for a 36-card pack, the 5s are also removed; for a 32-card pack, the 6s are also removed.

The suits in most games are of equal value, but some games, as explained in the main text, grade the suits in order of importance. So far as the ranks of individual cards are concerned, in most games the cards are ranked in importance as set out in the list above, with the Ace the highest ranked. Originally, the Ace was the one and ranked lowest, but early in the history of card games (ie before 1500) the Ace began to take precedence over all others. In some games, however, the old order stands, and Ace counts as the lowest card. Some games, especially those which originate in continental Europe, have eccentric rankings of the cards, particularly regarding 10s and 2s. Rankings are given, where appropriate, in the descriptions of all the games in the main text.

Deciding partnerships
In games of four players requiring partnerships, respective partners can be decided by mutual agreement or by chance. If by chance is preferred, the usual method is for any player to shuffle the cards and another to cut (see Shuffling and Cutting, below). Each player then cuts the pack, with the two players cutting the lowest cards forming a partnership against the two highest. The lowest of all is the dealer and he chooses his seat with his partner sitting opposite. Any variations from this practice are mentioned in the individual descriptions of games.

Rotation of play
In most games the right to deal, the order of bidding and the turn to play rotate to the left, ie clockwise. However, in some games originating in continental Europe the converse is true, and play rotates to the right, ie anti-clockwise.

Shuffling
A safe way to shuffle the pack is to place it on the table, and divide it roughly into two by taking the top half and placing it end to end with the lower half. Then, holding the two halves

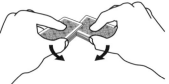

abutting each other, riffle them together by running the thumbs up the sides of each half while holding the two packs firm with the fingers on the opposite edge, as shown in the second illustration. With the two halves interleaved, slide them together as in the third illustration. Then, take about a third of the cards from the top and place the bottom two-thirds on top of them. Repeat the whole process twice more, not forgetting the final cut, and the pack should be well shuffled.

Cutting

There are two types of cut. In the cut whereby each player cuts the pack to determine partners or who deals, the player merely takes a packet of cards from the top of the pack, which should be face down on the table, and turns it over to expose the bottom card.

The cut made before another player deals has another purpose. It is the final insurance that the pack has not been arranged. In this cut, the player takes a packet from the top of the face-down pack (the packet should be of at least five cards), places it on the table face down and places what was previously the lower part of the pack on top of it.

Dealing

It is customary before the deal for the pack to be shuffled by the dealer. Although any player may ask to shuffle prior to the dealer, the dealer has the right to shuffle last. He then places the pack face down before his right-hand neighbour, who cuts it as described above. It is in order for this player merely to take a packet from the top of the pack and place it on the table, leaving the dealer to complete the cut by placing the lower portion on top. It is open for a player to refuse to cut, in which case any other player may volunteer. If none wishes to, the dealer must cut the cards himself. This description is for games where the play rotates to the left; in games where play rotates anti-clockwise, the left-hand neighbour of the dealer cuts.

The dealer deals the cards, in nearly all games face down, to each player in turn, either one at a time or in packets as the game requires, until all players have the required number. It is customary and courteous for players to wait until the deal is complete before touching their cards (see also Customs, Practices and Etiquette, p157).

Misdealing

If there is a misdeal, which can occur for various reasons, such as a card being turned face up, or being already face up in the pack, or there being cards missing, the cards must be gathered up and the dealer must begin again. However, if there is an advantage in being the dealer, then the misdealer loses the deal, which passes to the next player.

Trumps and tricks

Many games involve taking 'tricks'. A trick is a round of play to which each player contributes a card. The usual rule (and one must emphasize the *usual* rule) is that all players must follow suit to the card led, eg if the leader (the player who contributes the first card to the trick) leads a heart, all other players must contribute a heart if they are able to, ie if they hold a heart in their hand. If a player does not hold a card of the suit led, he must play any other card. The card which wins the trick is the highest card that it contains of the suit led.

However, in most trick-taking games, there is a 'trump' suit, which is decided by various different methods according to the rules of the game being played. The word 'trump' is a corruption of 'triumph', and a card from the trump suit triumphs over one from any other suit. Thus, where there is a trump suit, a player who does not hold a card of the suit led, but who does hold a card of the trump suit, may play the trump, which will win the trick, unless a subsequent player who is also devoid of a card in the suit led plays a higher trump. Thus, a trick is won by the highest trump it contains, or if it does not contain a trump, by the highest card in the suit led.

A player's first obligation is to play a card in the suit led. If he is unable to, he may play a trump, thus beating all cards of the suit led. He is not allowed to play a trump if he holds a card of the suit led. On the other hand, if he does not hold a card of the suit led, he is not obliged to play a trump – he may play any other card (called a 'discard'). A discard, of course, can never win a trick. A player is not obliged to try to win a trick.

To sum up: the leader plays a card of a certain suit (which may or may not be a trump). Subsequent players must follow suit if they can, and if they cannot may play a trump or discard as they wish. The highest trump wins the trick – if none is played the highest card of the suit led wins.

This is what is meant by the phrase often used in this book: 'the normal rules of trick-taking apply'.

Of course, inevitably there are games where the normal rules do not apply. In these games it might be compulsory to trump, or it might be that you can trump even if holding a card of the suit led, or it might even be that it is not obligatory to follow suit to the card led. In all games where these deviations from the normal rules apply they are carefully explained in the individual descriptions of play.

Duration of play

It is important in games where money is changing hands, to agree a time when play will stop, or at least a time when any player who wishes to leave the game may do so. This saves a lot of hard feeling in games where players who are winning feel obliged to play for longer than they wish because losing players insist on nobody leaving while they themselves are losing.

Card Games Glossary

The glossary does not include game names or variants, for which the index can be consulted.

abundance in Solo Whist, an undertaking to win nine tricks

abundance declared in Solo Whist, an undertaking to win all thirteen tricks

royal abundance in Solo Whist, an undertaking to win nine tricks with the turn-up suit as trumps

all in in Texas Hold 'Em, to have all your chips in the pot

ante (a) in Brag and Poker, a compulsory stake put down by a player before the deal (b) a contribution to a pot before the deal which belongs to all players

auction the period in which bidding takes place

avec la table in Chemin de Fer, a call which allows a player to bet half the value of the amount in the bank

banco (a) in Chemin de Fer, a call which allows a player to bet the whole of the amount in the bank (b) in Punto Banco, a bet on the bank rather than the players

banco suivi in Chemin de Fer, a call which allows a player to bet the whole of the amount in the bank, having already made and lost a bet of banco

bank an amount of chips or coins put up by a banker for players to bet against

banker a person who keeps or acts as the bank (sometimes representing the casino)

basto in Ombre, ♣A, which is always a trump

beg in All Fours, as the non-dealer, to decline the turn-up card as trumps

bid an offer to make a certain number of tricks or points in play

bidding the act or process of making bids, or the bids made

blackjack in Blackjack, a two-card combination of an Ace and a ten-point card, giving a value of 21 points

blind bets in Texas Hold 'Em, small compulsory stakes put in by the first two players to the left of the dealer

big blind in Texas Hold 'Em, a small compulsory stake put in by the second player to the left of the dealer, larger than that put in by the first player to the left of the dealer

small blind in Texas Hold 'Em, a small compulsory stake put in by the first player to the left of the dealer

blind betting making a bet without seeing the cards held

blücher in Napoleon, an optional extra bid to win all five tricks, bid only after a previous player has bid wellington

bluff usually in Poker, to seek to deceive by betting as if you have a stronger or weaker hand than you really hold

bragger in Classical Brag, one of three wild cards: ♦A, ♣J or ♦9

burn to discard a card without its value being shown, usually prior to a deal

burying in Pinochle, the laying away face down by the bidder, after taking the widow, of any three cards not used in a meld

bust in Pontoon, to exceed the score of 21 when drawing cards

button in Texas Hold 'Em, a disc moved round the table on each deal to indicate which player is the 'dealer' and thus which players must put in the blinds

buy in Pontoon, to receive a card face down, for a stake not exceeding the original stake

call in Poker, to make a bet exactly equal to the previous bet

capture to win possession of a card during play, thus taking it into the hand or scoring points from it

card one of a pack, usually of 52 cards, divided into four suits used in playing games

boodle card a card on which coins or chips are placed which can be won by players

card sharp, card sharper a person who cheats at cards

community card in Poker, a card that can be used by any player to help form a hand

court card the King, Queen or Jack of each suit

face card *same as* court card

guarded card a card in a suit in which lower-ranking cards are also held, eg a King which becomes master card when a lower card has been played on the Ace

high card in Brag and Poker, a hand lacking any combinations and thus ranked by the highest ranked card it contains

hole card in versions of Poker, eg Stud, a card dealt face down to a player

master card the highest card not yet played in a suit, and therefore the card that controls that suit

natural card a card that is not a Joker or a wild card

non-valle card in Panguingue, any card except the 7s, 5s and 3s

penalty card a card which brings a scoring or other disadvantage to the player who holds or wins it

picture card *same as* court card

plain card a card other than a court card

trump card a card turned up to determine the trump suit; any card of that suit, or a card otherwise designated a trump by the rules of the game

upcard the top card of a pile, turned face up

valle card in Panguingue, the 7s, 5s and 3s

wild card a card which can represent any card its holder wishes and which can be used in place of any other card

casino a gambling house

casino edge the percentage advantage that a casino has on the bets it offers and therefore the percentage it would expect to win over the long run

check in Poker, the option to stay in the deal without staking

chip a token of wood, plastic or similar, used to represent money

circle bet in Monte Bank, a bet on one rank to be matched before any of the other three in the layout

codille in Ombre, the situation in which one opponent wins more tricks than ombre

colour the colour of the pips and characters on a card: red for diamonds and hearts, black for spades and clubs

comet in Comet, the wildcards: ♦9 in the black pack and ♣9 in the red pack

condition in Panguingue, certain melds which allow a player to immediately collect chips from the other active players

contract an undertaking by a player or partnership to win a certain number of tricks

cop in Solo Whist, a call that signifies acceptance of a proposal bid

couleur in Trente et Quarante, a bet that the first card turned up will be the same colour as the winning row

counting out in All Fours, the scoring of enough points to win the game before the deal is played out

crisscross bet in Monte Bank, a bet on one rank to be matched before a certain other rank in the layout

croupier a person who officiates at a gaming table, collecting the stakes and paying the winners, and sometimes dealing

curse of Scotland ♦9

cut to divide a pack of cards by lifting the upper portion at random, either to expose a card or suit, or in order to replace the parts of the pack in a different order before dealing

dead hand an extra hand which plays no part in a game

deal (*a*) to distribute cards to each player, or the act of distributing cards (*b*) the period between one deal and the next, including bidding, playing, scoring etc

151

dealer a person who deals cards, or whose turn it is to deal, or who has dealt the hand in play

dealing shoe *same as* shoe

goulash deal a re-deal of cards without shuffling

deck *same as* pack

declaration a call or bid

declare to show cards in order to score

declarer in Napoleon, the highest bidder

deuce the 2 of each suit

die Alten *same as* old women

discard to throw away a card or cards, as not needed or not allowed by the game; to throw down a (useless) card of another suit when you cannot follow suit and cannot or will not trump; the act of discarding; the card or cards thrown out of the hand

dix in Pinochle, the 9 of trumps

double bête in Pinochle, the defeat of the bidder if he has scored fewer points than his contract

double down in Blackjack, an option for a player to double his stake and receive a third card face down

doubler bet in Monte Bank, a bet that one of a pair of ranks will be matched before one of the remaining two ranks in the layout

draw (*a*) to take a card from a face-down pack to determine seats, dealer etc (*b*) to take a card or cards from the stock, either to replace discards or to increase the number of cards held

draw trumps to repeatedly lead trumps in order to exhaust opponents' hands of trumps

dressing the board in Pope Joan, the placing of chips or coins by the dealer onto the board

drop out to cease to play any part in a game, either by choice or necessity

eighty Kings in Pinochle, the scoring combination of one King of each suit

elder, eldest hand the player on the dealer's left (or, in games of Spanish derivation, the player on the dealer's right)

expose to show the cards in a hand to other players or the banker

face the printed side of a playing card that shows its pip value, as opposed to the back

face down with the side of the card that displays the pip value hidden

face up with the side of the card that displays the pip value visible

false draws in Chemin de Fer, a practice in which both player and banker are allowed to draw or stand at their discretion

faux tirages *same as* false draws

fifth street in Poker, a final fifth card dealt to the row of community cards on the table in Texas Hold 'Em and Omaha

flop in Poker, the first three community cards dealt face up to the table in Texas Hold 'Em and Omaha

flush (*a*) a hand in which all the cards are of the same suit (*b*) in Pinochle, a meld of the Ace, 10, King, Queen and Jack of trumps

royal flush in Poker, a sequence of Ace, King, Queen, Jack and 10 of the same suit (the highest hand of all)

running flush in Brag, three cards in sequence of the same suit

straight flush in Poker, a sequence of five cards of the same suit

fold in Poker, to drop out

foot in Panguingue, the lower part of the stock

force to force an opponent to play a particular card, usually a trump

forty Jacks in Pinochle, the scoring combination of one Jack of each suit

four of a kind in Poker, four cards of the same rank with an unmatched card

fourth street in Poker, a fourth card dealt to the row of community cards on the table in Texas Hold 'Em and Omaha

freeze-out a game which cannot end until only two players are left in or a limit is reached

full house in Poker, three cards of one rank with two of another

game in All Fours, a point for winning the highest value of scoring cards in tricks

gate in Monte Bank, the bottom card of the pack when exposed

gift in All Fours, a point given to the non-dealer if the dealer wishes to accept the turn-up as trumps

go bust *same as* bust

go on top in Panguingue, a declaration made by a player to indicate he is dropping out by placing a forfeit on top of the foot of the stock

go out to win by getting rid of all the cards in a hand

group in Panguingue, a type of meld

guard a card or cards that protect a high card so that an opponent cannot win several instant tricks with a long suit

hand the set of cards held by a player at one deal; the play of a single deal of cards

hard in Blackjack, a hand which does not contain an Ace or which counts an Ace as one

head in Panguingue, the upper part of the stock

high in All Fours, a point for winning the highest trump in play

hit in Blackjack, a request for an additional free card (*cf* twist in Pontoon)

hundred Aces in Pinochle, the scoring combination of one Ace of each suit

in prison in Trente et Quarante, a stake left on the table after a refait

insurance in Blackjack, an optional bet offered to players by the banker when he has an Ace, showing that he will get a natural (thus saving the player his stake); in Trente et Quarante, the opportunity to insure against a refait with a payment of 1% of the stake

inverse in Trente et Quarante, a bet that the colour of the first card turned will be the opposite colour to that of the winning row

jack in All Fours, a point for winning the Jack of trumps

jinking it in Spoil Five, an undertaking by a player who has won three tricks to take the last two tricks as well

joint soloist in Solo Whist, one of the players in temporary partnership in a proposal and acceptance bid

Joker a 53rd or 54th card in the pack, used in some games

kicker in Poker, an unpaired card that determines which of two otherwise equivalent hands wins the pot

kitty *same as* pool

knave a Jack

lay off in Panguingue, to add cards to one's own meld

le grand in Baccarat, a two-card hand with a point of 9

le petit in Baccarat, a two-card hand with a point of 8

lead to play the first card of a round or trick; the first card laid

looed in Loo, applied to a player who played but failed to win a trick

low in All Fours, a point for winning the lowest trump in play

make to declare as trumps; to win a trick

manille in Ombre, the 7 of trumps when a red suit is trumps or the 2 of trumps when a black suit is trumps

marriage in Pinochle, a scoring combination of King and Queen

common marriage in Pinochle, the scoring combination of the King and Queen of a plain suit

royal marriage in Pinochle, the scoring combination of the King and Queen of trumps

matador in Ombre, one of the three top trumps: spadille, manille and basto

meld a combination or group of scoring cards, usually three or more of the same rank, or of the same suit and in sequence; to show or announce such a group

mis *same as* misère

misdeal any departure from the correct procedure in dealing

misère an undertaking to lose all the tricks

153

misère ouvert in Solo Whist, an undertaking to lose all the tricks, with the hand exposed on the table for opponents to see after the first trick has been played

open misère *same as* misère ouvert

miss in Loo, an extra hand

nap same as napoleon

napoleon in Napoleon, a bid to win all five possible tricks

natural (*a*) a set or sequence of cards containing no wild cards (*b*) in Blackjack, *same as* blackjack (*c*) in Baccarat, Chemin de Fer and Punto Banco, a two-card hand with a point of 9 or 8 (*d*) in Classical Brag, a scoring combination without a bragger (*e*) in Pontoon, *same as* pontoon

natural 8 *same as* le petit

natural 9 *same as* le grand

noir in Trente et Quarante, black, or the row representing it

non-dealer in a two-handed game, the player who is not currently acting as the dealer

old women in Schafkopf, the two black Queens

ombre in Ombre, the player who has the right to name the trump suit and to exchange cards by discarding and drawing from the stock

one-eyed Jack ♥J or ♠J

pack a complete set of playing cards, usually comprising 52 cards

Italian pack a pack of cards traditionally used in Italy, comprising 40 cards

Spanish pack a pack of cards traditionally used in Spain, comprising 40 cards

pair two cards of the same rank

no pair in Poker, *same as* high card

one pair in Poker, a hand of two cards of one rank plus three unmatched cards

open pair in Stud Poker, a pair among a player's cards face up on the table

pair-royal three cards of the same rank

pam in Five-Card Loo, ♣J

partnership a team of two, or occasionally more, players

pass to abstain from making a bid, declaration or other play

pat hand in Poker, a hand whose holder does not wish to try to improve by drawing

pinochle in Pinochle, ♠Q and ♦J

pip a suit symbol spot on a card

pip value the total of the pips on a playing card, for example a 3 card has a pip value of 3

playing over in Pinochle, the requirement that each player must, if able, play a higher trump than any previously played if a trump is led

playing the board in Texas Hold 'Em, choosing to use neither of the two hole cards held in a hand

pontoon in Pontoon, a two-card hand of 21, consisting of an Ace and a 10-count card

pool the collective stakes of a number of players, which can be won during the game

scoop the pool to win the total amount of money in the pool

pot *same as* pool

preferential bet in Baccarat, a bet of banco, banco suivi or avec la table

prial (*a*) in Brag, three cards of the same rank (*b*) in Pontoon, a hand of three 7s

prop in Solo Whist, a proposal bid

proposal in Solo Whist, a bid that asks for a partner with whom to make eight tricks with the turn-up as trumps

puesta in Ombre, the situation in which one or both opponents wins the same number of tricks as ombre, with ombre doubling the amount in the pool and the doubled pool being carried forward to the next deal

punto (*a*) in Punto Banco, a bet on the players rather than the bank (*b*) in Ombre, the Ace of trumps when a red suit is trumps

raise in Poker, to put in an amount equal to the previous stake plus a further amount to raise the stake higher

rank the grade or position of a particular card in its suit, for example 3, 10 or Jack are ranks

refait in Trente et Quarante, an occasion in which both rows of cards tie at 31

refusal in All Fours, the rejection by the dealer of a beg (ie the refusal to allow the eldest hand to score for gift)

renege *same as* revoke

renounce *same as* revoke

revoke (*a*) to fail to follow suit when able to, and required to by the rules (*b*) to play a card which contravenes the rules of the game

rouge in Trente et Quarante, red, or the row representing it

ruff *same as* trump

run in Brag, three cards in sequence

run the cards in All Fours, to discard the initial turn-up, deal three extra cards to each player and turn up a new card as the trump indicator

sabot *same as* shoe

sacardo in Ombre, a situation in which ombre takes more tricks than either of his opponents and hence takes the pool

schneider in Schafkopf, to take more than 90 points in tricks

schneidered in Schafkopf, applied to a losing side which failed to score 31 points in tricks

schwarz in Schafkopf, winning all the tricks

sequence a set of three or more cards consecutive in value

sharper *same as* card sharp

shoe a box-like device for dispensing cards singly

short pack, shortened pack a pack which has been reduced from 52 cards to some other number by the removal of all cards of a certain rank or ranks

showdown in Poker, the exposure of players' cards face up on the table at the end of a game

shuffle to mix cards at random

single bête in Pinochle, the concession of defeat by the bidder without leading to a trick

sixty Queens in Pinochle, the scoring combination of one Queen of each suit

sleeping applied to a card or cards not in play

soft in Blackjack, a hand which counts an Ace as eleven

solo (*a*) in Solo Whist, an undertaking to make five tricks with the turn-up suit as trumps (*b*) a bid to play without using a widow or without help of a partner

spadille in Ombre, ♠A, the highest trump

spin, spinado in Spinado, ♦A

split in Blackjack, to divide a hand of two cards of the same rank into two separate hands

spoiled in Spoil Five, applied to a hand in which nobody wins three tricks

spread in Panguingue, a meld of three cards

stake money or chips staked on an outcome not yet known; to deposit as a wager

maximum stake the highest amount of coins and chips which players may contribute in a gambling game

minimum stake the lowest amount of coins and chips which players are obliged to contribute in a gambling game

stand (*a*) in Blackjack, to keep a hand unchanged, rather than drawing another card in the hope of improving it (*b*) in All Fours, as the non-dealer, to accept the turn-up card as trumps

stand pat in Poker, to play a hand as it was dealt, without drawing any cards

stay in Poker, to remain in the game without raising

stick in Pontoon, a declaration that a player is happy with his count and will not take any more cards

stock the undealt part of a pack of cards, which may be used later in the deal

stop in Newmarket and Pope Joan, an interruption of play caused by the required next card in the sequence not being in play

straight in Poker, a hand of five cards in sequence, but not of the same suit

straight flush in Poker, a hand of five cards in sequence and of the same suit

stringer in Panguingue, three cards of the same suit in sequence

suit one of the sets of cards of the same denomination: clubs, diamonds, hearts or spades

bare suit a suit of which no cards are held in a hand

follow suit to play a card of the same suit as the one which was led

long suit the suit with most cards in a hand, or a suit with a large number of cards held in a hand

plain suit a suit other than the trump suit

side suit *same as* plain suit

suited in Poker, hole cards of the same suit

suit of preference in Preference, the hearts suit

trump suit a suit that ranks higher than any other suit

tableau in Baccarat, the cards on the table upon which players may bet

Table of Play in Baccarat and its variants, a chart which sets out the best option for play in any given situation

talon *same as* widow

the river *same as* fifth street

three of a kind in Poker, a hand of three cards of the same rank with two unmatching cards

trick a round of play at cards, in which each player contributes one card; the cards so played and taken by the winner

overtrick a trick in excess of the number specified in a contract

undertrick a trick short of the number specified in a contract

trump, trumps a suit that ranks higher than any other suit, so that any card of this suit ranks higher than any card of the other three suits; a card of this suit; to play a trump card instead of following suit

trump indicator the card turned up to determine the trump suit

turn *same as* fourth street

twist in Pontoon, the option for a player to receive a further card face up, for which he does not pay

two pairs in Poker, two cards of one rank, two of another and an unmatched card

unlimited in Loo, a version of the game which obliges a player looed to put chips into the pool for the following deal equivalent to the amount of the pool at the beginning of the deal

void the total absence of cards of a particular suit in a hand

wellington in Napoleon, a bid to win all five tricks called only after a previous player has bid nap

widow an extra hand, which in some games may not be used, and in others may be added in entirety or in part to a player's hand

Customs, Practices and Etiquette

Apart from the actual rules of individual card games, described in the main text in this book under each game, and the common elements of card games, such as the cards themselves, choosing partners, shuffling, dealing and so on, which are dealt with in the section Card Games Basics on p147, there is another aspect surrounding games which is not much discussed or written about. This concerns the customs and etiquette of playing at cards, which if observed make the enjoyment of them greater.

With gambling games, the utmost care must be taken to ensure that all players obey the rules scrupulously, and there must be no doubt that everything is above board. Even gambling games which are played for small stakes, and principally for enjoyment, should also be taken seriously. Thus certain rules of etiquette have been established which should be observed if all players are to find the game enjoyable. Informality is fine, but players who are too interested in gossip to remember the rules, or whose lead it is, or which suit is trumps, should perhaps be occupied in some other amusement. A brief list of things to be avoided follows.

Playing or bidding out of turn
Nothing is more annoying than a player in a trick-taking game who leads out of turn. If it is a partnership game the lead out of turn conveys sometimes valuable – and always illegal – information to the partner of the offender.

When another player has led to a trick, a player might know immediately which card he will play (he might have no option), but absent-mindedly playing it before it is his turn is more than irritating – it can influence a player who should have played previously to change the card he would have played. In games where there is an auction, players should take care not to bid out of turn, as this illegally conveys information to a partner.

Picking up the cards as they are dealt
The dealer should be allowed to finish dealing before any players pick up their cards. Picking up the cards prematurely is not only considered bad manners, but the removal of cards mid-deal could lead the dealer to miss out the hand next round, causing a misdeal. Also, if all players pick up their hands together they have a similar time to consider them before play begins.

Chatting during play
This leads to a general lack of concentration all round and causes mistakes and annoyance. Between deals is fine for a little chatting, but the game should not be merely a background to gossip, and real scandal should be aired before the game (after all, nobody wants to wait until afterwards).

Playing a card and then asking for it back
Players should consider which card to play and play it smoothly. Do not ask for it back, as (in the words of notices in shops warning customers not to ask for credit) 'a refusal may offend'.

Commenting on the play
This falls into many categories. Comments which convey information to a partner are obviously unacceptable, but some players do not realize that innocent remarks can convey information.

Picking up a hand and saying 'this looks promising' could be enough to affect how other players play their hands. 'Don't rely on me, partner!' certainly will. Under this heading could come the fault of making statements which are necessary (as in bidding) in such a manner as to convey information, eg appearing to bid reluctantly. It is also irritating when players comment on another player's play, particularly if the comment is critical. And knowing remarks, such as 'I know who's got the Ace', are very annoying, not least to players who do not know who's got the Ace.

Gesturing

If passing information to other players by saying things out of turn or in a certain manner is not acceptable, it follows that doing the same thing with gestures is also to be discouraged. Frowning, shrugging, winking and sighing are not part of the game.

Playing too slowly

There is a line to be drawn between taking a game seriously and agonizing over every card played, to the extent that other players get impatient. Of course, playing too quickly, without any thought at all (and therefore probably playing badly) is just as annoying.

When sitting down to play cards, each player should appreciate that this is what they have decided to do, in preference to watching television, say. They owe it to the other players to concentrate on the game and play their part. Playing cards is not like knitting, which can be performed while thinking of something else. These rules of etiquette are all based on common sense and do not preclude conviviality, gossip between hands, glasses of wine or whatever else you want to do among family and friends. Win gracefully and lose sportingly.

Card Sharp's Guide

Cheating at cards is a fascinating subject, but not one that many people take seriously. Paintings of card games that show players slipping Aces under the table for use later, or sticking them in their belts or up their sleeves, are usually viewed with amusement. After all, this is not something that happens in your own household while playing with family and friends. And if you do sometimes get irritated with the friend who casually takes a peek at the bottom card while shuffling or cutting – well, he's probably doing it unconsciously and not meaning to cheat.

The average card player would be surprised at some of the apparatus that can be bought specially to aid cheating. How about a little reflector, with a hinge that opens and shuts like a ladies' compact, which can be easily attached to the underside of a table so that when opened the projecting reflector allows a dealer to see each card he deals? Or, if this seems cumbersome, a pipe with a tiny mirror in the bowl, which left casually on the table with the bowl facing the dealer gives him the same advantage (of course, the pipe's no good for smoking)? A ring for the finger which has a tiny point projecting from the underside will enable its owner to prick a tiny hole in any card or cards he wishes to recognize each time they appear in a deal. And a tiny dye box, like a button, to be sewn to clothing will, if touched with the finger which then touches the back of a card, leave a smudge of dye on the card just sufficient to allow it to be spotted easily from then on.

These are ways of marking cards during a game, but it is better to play with cards already marked. Card manufacturers do not make marked cards, but there are gambling supply houses which will mark packs made by standard manufacturers and reseal them. However, it is easy enough to mark cards yourself. Even cards which have complicated designs on the back (or, perhaps, especially these cards) can easily be marked with spots or lines added in carefully selected places, using ink which more or less matches the colour of the design. It is not necessary to be too subtle about it, since how often do other players examine the backs of cards to check if there are marks? On the other hand, cards can be marked so skilfully that the marks will stand out to the marker who put them there but will be difficult to find by another player even if he were told they were there.

Rather than adding marks to cards it is possible, with a razor blade, to scrape off minute areas of the pattern to make them instantly recognizable. Of course, a card marker needs to mark both ends of the card in identical fashion, so that he can recognize the mark no matter from which end he is viewing it.

The poor card marker finding himself in a game with honest cards and no apparatus or dye to mark them as he goes along need not despair. Digging his thumbnail halfway up each side edge of an Ace will enable him to spot it whenever it is dealt. A thumbnail dig three-quarters of the way up will help him spot the Kings. Imagine the advantage to a player of Texas Hold 'Em or Stud Poker if he knows how many Aces or Kings are among the hole cards of his opponents.

More sophisticated cheating involves false shuffles, palming or dealing from the bottom of the pack. A swindle many will have seen is the Three-Card Trick, or Find the Lady. This was often practised by gangs at race tracks, and can employ both sleight of hand and marking. Three cards are shown to the 'punters', one of which is a Queen. They are laid on a portable

table and the audience invited to bet on which is the Queen (ie they are invited to 'find the lady'). It looks so obvious which card is the Queen, but anyone foolish enough to put his money down will certainly lose it, as a neat bit of sleight of hand has switched the positions of the cards (if somebody does get it right, it will be an accomplice of the operator). Occasionally the Queen will be seen to have a corner of the card creased. How can you then go wrong? Down goes the money on the creased card, only for the punter to find that somehow it has become a completely different card, with an identical crease in the corner. A reference to a version of this swindle has been discovered in court records in France dated 1408. By the way, the Find the Lady trick is operated by gangs. Do not become too interested, even academically, without keeping your hand on your wallet, since picking pockets is a well-known secondary source of income for the operators.

For the cards used at home, little guillotines can be bought to trim playing cards. The backs of playing cards are often printed with patterns centred on the card, leaving a white margin at the edges of around 4 mm. Trimming one millimetre from one side of all the Aces will make the pattern on the back so off-centre as to make them immediately recognizable to one who knows what to look for. Of course, to disguise the trimming you have to trim half a millimetre off each side of all the other cards to make all the cards the same width, but this is no problem to a dedicated cheat.

Of course, you can cheat with perfectly legitimate cards and no sleight of hand by having an accomplice. When casinos were introduced into Britain, the Gaming Board restricted the options offered to players and the dealer at Blackjack, partly to reduce the house edge against poor players, but also to prevent the possibility of the dealer cheating in collusion with a player by indicating to him the value of his face-down card, which is a scam casinos have always had to look out for. In private games, of course, it is the 'kibitzer', or casual onlooker, who can easily pass information about one player's hand to another who might be his friend.

In card games where players have partners, it is not difficult or unknown for players to pass information secretly to one another, and indeed in the 1965 World Bridge championships, two of the world's leading players were convicted by the World Bridge Federation of signalling to each other the number of cards each held in the heart suit by means of how they held the cards in their hands. This would be very valuable information for experts. After a later special inquiry, both players were acquitted of any wrongdoing.

One of the most famous instances of cheating occurred in 1890 when, at a private house party during the St Leger race meeting, the Prince of Wales – later Edward VII – decided to play Baccarat. Although the Prince possessed his own cloth and counters with which he travelled, the game was then illegal. Some of the players suspected the Prince's friend, Sir William Gordon-Cumming, of cheating by manipulating his betting counters after the result was known. In a subsequent session he was watched carefully, the suspicions confirmed, and the information passed to the Prince, who forbade him to play. Later, when the story began to circulate in society, Sir William sued for slander, and the Prince was forced to give evidence in the witness box, and admit to illegal gambling, which did not amuse Queen Victoria.

Cheating at cards is clearly something that can happen in the highest circles, but is not advocated, and this section is provided, like card games themselves, for amusement only.

Index

Games by Alternative Names

American Brag *see* Brag **28**
Auction Solo *see* Solo Whist **123**

Baccara *see* Baccarat **10**
Blackjack *see* Pontoon **99**
Blind Hookey *see* Banker **18**
Boodle *see* Newmarket **63**

Chemin de Fer *see* Baccarat **10**
Chicago *see* Newmarket **63**
Classical Brag *see* Brag **28**
Commit *see* Comet **34**

Dealer's Choice *see* Poker **81**
Down the River *see* Poker **81**
Draw Poker *see* Poker **81**
Dutch Bank *see* Banker **18**

English Roulette
    see Hoggenheimer **42**
English Seven-card Stud *see* Poker **81**

Five-card Loo *see* Loo **51**
Five-card Stud Poker *see* Poker **81**

High-card Pool *see* Red Dog **113**
High-Low-Jack *see* All Fours **5**
High-Low Poker *see* Poker **81**
Hold 'Em *see* Poker **81**
Hombre *see* Ombre **66**
Horse Race *see* Racing **110**

Irish Loo *see* Loo **51**

Jackpots *see* Poker **81**
Jewish Faro *see* Stuss **135**

Lowball *see* Poker **81**

Maw *see* Spoil Five **131**
Michigan *see* Newmarket **63**

Nap *see* Napoleon **59**
Nine-card Brag *see* Brag **28**

Old Sledge *see* All Fours **5**
Omaha *see* Poker **81**
Omaha High-Low Eight *see* Poker **81**

Pan *see* Panguingue **71**
Progressive Jackpots *see* Poker **81**
Punto Banco *see* Baccarat **10**

Rocamber *see* Ombre **66**
Rouge et Noir *see* Trente et
    Quarante **142**

Saratoga *see* Newmarket **63**
Schnautz *see* Thirty-One **140**
Seven-card Brag *see* Brag **28**
Seven-card Stud *see* Poker **81**
Seven-toed Pete *see* Poker **81**
Seven-Up *see* All Fours **5**
Shoot *see* Slippery Sam **120**
Simple Brag *see* Brag **28**
Spanish Monte *see* Monte Bank **55**
Spin *see* Spinado **128**
Spit in the Ocean *see* Poker **81**
Stops *see* Newmarket **63**
Stud Poker *see* Poker **81**

Texas Hold 'Em *see* Poker **81**
Three-stake Brag *see* Brag **28**
Trentacinque *see* Thirty-Five **137**
Trente-et-Un *see* Thirty-One **140**
Tresillo *see* Ombre **66**
Twenty-Five *see* Spoil Five **131**
Twenty-One *see* Pontoon **99**

Unlimited Loo *see* Loo **51**

Vingt-et-Un *see* Pontoon **99**
Vingt-Un *see* Pontoon **99**

Games by Number of Players

Games for One or Two Players

Games that can be played by a single player against a banker in a casino are marked *.

Ace-Deuce-Jack 3
All Fours 5
Baccarat* 10
Banker 18
Blackjack* 20
Brag 28
Comet 34
Crazy Eights 37
Easy Go 39
Hoggenheimer 42

Lansquenet 45
Le Truc 48
Napoleon 59
Panguingue* 71
Poker 81
Spinado 128
Spoil Five 131
Stuss 135
Thirty-Five 137
Trente et Quarante* 142

Games for Three Players

Ace-Deuce-Jack 3
All Fours (variants) 5
Baccarat 10
Bango 16
Banker 18
Blackjack 20
Blücher 26
Brag 28
Comet (variants) 34
Crazy Eights 37
Easy Go 39
Hoggenheimer 42
Lansquenet 45
Loo 51
Monte Bank 55
Napoleon 59
Newmarket 63

Ombre 66
Panguingue 71
Pinochle 75
Poker 81
Pontoon 99
Pope Joan 104
Preference 107
Racing 110
Red Dog 113
Slippery Sam 120
Spinado 128
Spoil Five 131
Stuss 135
Thirty-Five 137
Thirty-One 140
Trente et Quarante 142

Games for Four Players

Ace-Deuce-Jack 3
All Fours (variants) 5
Baccarat 10
Bango 16
Banker 18
Blackjack 20
Blücher 26
Brag 28

Comet (variants) 34
Crazy Eights 37
Easy Go 39
Hoggenheimer 42
Lansquenet 45
Loo 51
Monte Bank 55
Napoleon 59

Newmarket 63
Panguingue 71
Pinochle (variants) 75
Poker 81
Pontoon 99
Pope Joan 104
Racing 110
Red Dog 113
Schafkopf 116

Slippery Sam 120
Solo Whist 123
Spinado 128
Spoil Five 131
Stuss 135
Thirty-Five 137
Thirty-One 140
Trente et Quarante 142

Games for Five or More Players

Ace-Deuce-Jack 3
Baccarat 10
Bango 16
Banker 18
Blackjack 20
Blücher 26
Brag 28
Comet (variants) 34
Crazy Eights 37
Easy Go 39
Hoggenheimer 42
Lansquenet 45
Loo 51
Monte Bank 55
Napoleon 59

Newmarket 63
Panguingue 71
Pinochle (variants) 75
Poker 81
Pontoon 99
Pope Joan 104
Racing 110
Red Dog 113
Slippery Sam 120
Spinado 128
Spoil Five 131
Stuss 135
Thirty-Five 137
Thirty-One 140
Trente et Quarante 142

Games by Type

Banking Games
Ace-Deuce-Jack 3
Baccarat 10
Banker 18
Blücher 26
Hoggenheimer 42
Lansquenet 45
Monte Bank 55
Pontoon 99
Racing 110
Slippery Sam 120
Stuss 135

Casino Games
Baccarat 10
Blackjack 20
Panguingue 71
Poker 81
Trente et Quarante 142

Chance Games
Ace-Deuce-Jack 3
Bango 16
Banker 18
Crazy Eights 37
Easy Go 39
Lansquenet 45
Monte Bank 55
Racing 110
Stuss 135
Thirty-Five 137
Trente et Quarante 142

Pool Games
Bango 16
Crazy Eights 37
Easy Go 39
Loo 51
Monte Bank 55
Newmarket 63
Ombre 66
Pope Joan 104
Preference 107
Red Dog 113
Schafkopf 116
Spinado 128
Spoil Five 131
Thirty-Five 137
Thirty-One 140

Stops Games
Comet 34
Newmarket 63
Pope Joan 104
Spinado 128

Trick-taking Games
All Fours 5
Le Truc 48
Loo 51
Napoleon 59
Ombre 66
Pinochle 75
Preference 107
Schafkopf 116
Solo Whist 123
Spoil Five 131

Chambers & Card Games

Chambers Card Games

Chambers Card Games is a comprehensive and fun guide to 100 varied card games, suitable for players of all ages and for any occasion. As well as providing detailed instructions, strategies and tips, this fully-illustrated book also features a history of card games and the stories behind the court cards.

Whether you're playing cards alone or with friends and family, for profit or just for pleasure, this book contains everything you need to know for hours of entertainment.

Price: £9.99   *ISBN: 978 0550 10336 9*
Paperback   *420 pages*

Chambers Pocket Card Games

This compact new collection features dozens of great card games, with clear instructions backed up by illustrations, strategies and handy hints, as well as practical information to help novice players get started. From bezique on the beach to patience on the plane, *Chambers Pocket Card Games* is an ideal travel companion as well as a useful home reference.

Price: £5.99   *ISBN: 978 0550 10408 3*
Paperback   *288 pages*

Chambers Card Games For One

Players of all ages and levels of skill will find
something to enjoy in this diverse collection of more
than 60 patience games. *Chambers Card Games
for One* includes classic favourites as well as more
unusual games, ranging from easy-to-play
Accordion and Clock to the more challenging
Flower Garden and Miss Milligan. Perfect for a rainy
afternoon or a solo trip.

Price: £5.99   *ISBN: 978 0550 10407 6*

Paperback   *176 pages*

Visit www.chambers.co.uk for further details, or call
0131 556 5929 for a Chambers catalogue.